J.M.J.

The Book of Gratitude

Seton Home Study School
1350 Progress Drive
Front Royal, VA 22630

Table of Contents

Title	Page
Bethlehem	1
Velvet Shoes	2
How Gloosksap Found the Summer	3-6
The Christmas Candle	7
The Saint Who Laughed	8-10
Travel	11-12
God's World	13
The Ship	14
The Selfish Giant	15-22
The Lady and The Aztec	23-28
Madonna Remembers	29
Little Pear	30-38
Saint of the Sea	39-40
The Barefoot Boy	41-44
Lily of the Mohawks	45-48
Trees	49
Apostle of South America	50-53
Chī-weé and the Rabbit	54-63
An Indian Summer	64
Apostle of the North	65-68
The Golden Touch	69-77
Saints of the Wide Roads	78-80
White Fields	81
Holy Eve	82-91
How Far is it to Bethlehem	92
Stopping by Woods on a Snowy Evening	93

Song of the Brook _____ 94-95
Ships _____ 96
The First Saint of the Americas _____ 97-100
The Ships of Yule _____ 101-102
The First Birthday _____ 103-108
A Carol for Sleepy Children _____ 109
The Mountain Pasture _____ 110-115
In the Fields _____ 115
Easter _____ 116
Sheep and the Lamb _____ 117
How Phidias Helped the Image-Maker _____ 118-123
Beautiful Things _____ 124
The Saint of Gardeners _____ 125-128
Petite Susanne _____ 129-136
The Canadian Pioneers _____ 137
The Wonderful Tar Baby _____ 138-142
Sea Shell _____ 143
If Once you Have Slept on an Island _____ 144
Black Beauty _____ 145-153
The Legend of the Christmas Rose _____ 154-156
Bells in the Country _____ 157
A Wish for Laughter _____ 158

Bethlehem

SISTER MADELEVA, C.S.C.

On Christmas Eve in Bethlehem town
The shadows fall; the night comes down;
The stars shine clear; the winds grow mild;
An inn stands open for a Child
On Christmas Eve in Bethlehem town.

In Bethlehem on Christmas day
One manger is fresh strewn with hay,
And you will find a young Child there,
And you will find a lady fair
In Bethlehem on Christmas day.

All roads must lead to Bethlehem,
All men at last must follow them,
And be you great or be you small
The sweet Lord Jesus bless you all
Upon the roads to Bethlehem.

Velvet Shoes

ELINOR WYLIE

Let us walk in the white snow
   In a soundless space;
With footsteps quiet and slow,
   At a tranquil pace,
   Under veils of white lace.

I shall go shod in silk,
   And you in wool,
White as a white cow's milk,
   More beautiful
   Than the breast of a gull.

We shall walk through the still town
   In a windless peace;
We shall step upon white down,
   Upon silver fleece,
   Upon softer than these.

We shall walk in velvet shoes:
   Wherever we go
Silence will fall like dews
   On white silence below.
   We shall walk in the snow.

Three hundred years ago the Micmac Indians of Nova Scotia built the first Catholic church in America to honor Saint Anne, their great patroness. But long before the missionaries came to Canada these Indians had worshiped the medicine man Glooskap, the myth of the North. One of their earlier beliefs is told in

How Glooskap Found the Summer

CHARLES GODFREY LELAND

In the long-ago time before the first white men came to live in the New World, a mighty race of Indians lived in the northeastern part of the New World. They called themselves Children of Light. Glooskap was their lord and master. He was ever kind to his people and did many great works for them.

Once, in Glooskap's day, it grew very cold; snow and ice were everywhere, fires would not give enough warmth; the corn would not grow and his people were perishing with cold and famine. Then Glooskap went very far north where all was ice. He came to a wigwam in which he found a giant, a great giant—for he was Winter. It was his icy breath that had frozen all the land. Glooskap entered the wigwam and sat down. Then Winter gave him a pipe and, as he smoked, the giant told tales of the olden times when he, Winter, reigned everywhere; when all the land was silent, white, and beautiful. The charm fell upon Glooskap; it was the frost charm. As the giant talked on and on, Glooskap fell asleep; and for six months he slept like a bear. Then the charm fled, as he was too strong for it, and he awoke.

3

Soon after he awoke, his talebearer, Tatler the Loon, a wild bird who lived on the shores of the lakes, brought him strange news. He told of a country far off to the south where it was always warm. There lived a Queen, who could easily overcome the giant, Winter. So Glooskap, to save his people, decided to go and find the Queen. Far off to the seashore he went and sang the magic song which the whales obey. Up came his old friend, Blob the Whale. She was Glooskap's carrier and bore him on her back when he wished to go far out to sea. Now the whale always had a strange law for travelers. She said to Glooskap, "You must shut your eyes tight while I carry you. To open them is dangerous. If you do that, I am sure to go aground on a reef or a sandbar and cannot get off, and you may be drowned."

Glooskap got on her back, and for many days the whale swam, and each day the water grew warmer and the air more balmy and sweet, for it came from spicy shores.

Soon they found themselves in shallow waters. Down in the sand the clams were singing a song of warning. "O big Whale," they sang, "keep out to sea, for the water here is shallow."

The whale said to Glooskap, who understood the language of all creatures, "What do they say?"

But Glooskap, wishing to land at once, said, "They tell you to hurry, for a storm is coming."

Then the whale hurried until she was close to the land, and Glooskap opened his left eye and peeped. At

once the whale stuck hard and fast on the beach, so that Glooskap, leaping from her head, walked ashore on dry land.

Far inland strode Glooskap, and at every step it grew warmer, and the flowers began to come up and talk with him. He came to where there were many fairies dancing in the forest. In the center of the group was one fairer than all the others. Her long, brown hair was crowned with flowers and her arms filled with blossoms. She was the Queen, Summer.

Glooskap knew that here at last was the Queen, who by her charms could melt old Winter's heart and force him to leave. He caught her up and kept her by a crafty trick. Glooskap cut a moose-hide into a long cord; as he ran away with Summer, he let the end trail behind him. The Fairies of Light pulled at the cord, but as Glooskap ran, the cord ran out, and though they pulled, he left them far behind.

So at last he came to the lodge of old Winter, but now he had Summer; and Winter welcomed him, for he hoped to freeze Glooskap to sleep again.

But this time Glooskap did the talking. This time his charm was the stronger, and before long the sweat ran down Winter's face. His icy tent melted. Then Summer used her strange power and everything awoke. The grass grew, the fairies came out, and the snow ran down the rivers, carrying away the dead leaves. Old Winter wept, seeing his power gone.

But Summer, the Queen, said to Winter, "I have proved that I am more powerful than you. I give you now all the country to the far North for your own, and there I shall never disturb you. Six months of every year you may come back to Glooskap's country and reign as of old, but you will be less severe. During the other six months, I myself will come from the South and rule the land."

Old Winter could do nothing but accept her offer. In the late autumn he comes back to Glooskap's country and reigns six months; but his rule is softer than in olden times. And when he comes, Summer runs home to the warm Southland. But at the end of six months, she always comes back to drive old Winter away to his own land, to awaken the northern land and to give it the joys that only she, the Queen, can give. And so, in Glooskap's old country, Winter and Summer, the cross old Giant and the beautiful Southern Queen, divide the rule of the land between them.

The Christmas Candle

BRIAN O'HIGGINS

In the name of God the Father,
  Of the Son and the Holy Ghost!
May the light of our Christmas Candle
  Reach those who will need it most.

We'll place it here in the window,
  And open the shutters wide,
And we'll pray for the ones who wander
  Through the gloom of the night outside.

We offer our prayer in memory
  Of that night long, long ago,
When Jesus and Mary and Joseph
  Were out in the wind and snow.

O bountiful Babe of Bethlehem!
  Look down on the homeless poor,
And lead their feet through the darkness
  Up here to our open door!

Where the kindly light of our candle
  Sheds forth a welcoming glow,
For the sake of the Gift God sent us
  One Christmas long ago.

The Saint Who Laughed

This is the story of the Saint who laughed.
His name was Philip Neri.
"I will have no sadness in my house," he said.
He laughed at his troubles. He laughed at his cat.
He laughed at life. He laughed at himself.

He thought that sin was folly.
So, to correct sin, he gave foolish penances.
Carry a big animal in your arms
through the streets of Rome!
Wear a great sign around your neck!
Sing a silly song in a public place!
Wear a fur coat in summer!
These were the penances he imposed.
Atonement over, he would ask the sinner,
"Now when do we begin to do good?"
Then he would laugh.

With his biretta cocked at a crazy angle,
His beard half-shaven and matted,
Philip Neri the nobleman,
Philip Neri the scholar,
Philip Neri, who cloaked his saintliness
in a garb of laughing humility,
tramped the streets of the holy city.
His mission was among the workshops of Rome,
the hospitals of Rome,
the Coliseum, where martyrs had died for the faith,
the homes of the poor.

The children of Rome loved Philip Neri.
He did not preach to them. He read aloud comic stories.
He played with the boys. He raced with them.
"How can you endure their noise?" a friend asked him.
"I would let these children chop wood upon my back," Philip said, "if it would serve to keep them innocent."

He spent his life in goodness and in charity,
and in laughter.
He spurned the world,
but no one in it.

The Spirit of God moved with him,
the spirit of joy,
the spirit of cheerfulness,
the spirit of kindness.

When Saint Philip Neri died
a tablet was placed upon the Janiculum,
one of the sunny hills of Rome
that looks down upon the everlasting beauty
of the immortal city.

In sunlight as bright as Philip Neri's smile
you can read the inscription:
"Here in the shade of this oak-tree,
amidst the merry shouts of boys,
Philip Neri—most wisely—became a boy again."

It is tribute to godliness.
It is tribute to laughter.

Travel

ROBERT LOUIS STEVENSON

I should like to rise and go
Where the golden apples grow;—
Where below another sky
Parrot islands anchored lie,
And, watched by cockatoos and goats,
Lonely Crusoes building boats;—
Where in sunshine reaching out
Eastern cities, miles about,
Are with mosque and minaret
Among sandy gardens set,
And the rich goods from near and far
Hang for sale in the bazaar;—
Where the Great Wall round China goes,
And on one side the desert blows,
And with bell and voice and drum,
Cities on the other hum;—
Where are forests, hot as fire,
Wide as England, tall as a spire,
Full of apes and coconuts
And the Negro hunters' huts;—
Where the knotty crocodile
Lies and blinks in the Nile,
And the red flamingo flies
Hunting fish before his eyes;—
Where in jungles, near and far,
Man-devouring tigers are,

Lying close and giving ear
Lest the hunt be drawing near,
Or a comer-by be seen
Swinging in a palanquin;—
Where among the desert sands
Some deserted city stands,
All its children, sweep and prince,
Of some dusty dining room;
Grown to manhood ages since,
Not a foot in street or house,
Not a stir of child or mouse,
And when kindly falls the night,
In all the town no spark of light.
There I'll come when I'm a man
With a camel caravan;
Light a fire in the gloom
See the pictures on the walls,
Heroes, fights, and festivals;
And in a corner find the toys
Of the old Egyptian boys.

God's World

HUGH FRANCIS BLUNT

There is a flower that blows
  On the desert wild,
Where no man ever goes:
  Oh, vain that flower smiled!
No man—yet God can see
How fair a flower may be.

There is a bird that sings
  In the woodland drear;
But trees are lifeless things—
  No man the song will hear.
No man—but God can tell
If birds are singing well.

The Ship

ROSE FYLEMAN

From the bay
I see a ship go by,
Far away
Against the golden sky.
What strange lands
She seeks I do not know—
What bright strands
Where radiant blossoms grow.

Lonely ship,
You vanish from my sight,
Soft you slip
Into the darkening night.
Who shall tell
What storms may throng your track?
Fare you well,
God send you safely back!

Once there was a garden to which spring never came.
How a little child made the birds sing
and the flowers blossom is the story of

The Selfish Giant

OSCAR WILDE

Every afternoon, as they were coming from school, the children used to go and play in the Giant's garden.

It was a large lovely garden with soft green grass. Here and there over the grass stood beautiful flowers like stars, and there were twelve peach trees that in the springtime broke out into delicate blossoms of pink and pearl, and in the autumn bore rich fruit. The birds sat in the trees and sang so sweetly that the children used to stop their games in order to listen to them. "How happy we are here!" they cried to each other.

One day the Giant came back. He had been to visit his friend, the Cornish ogre, and had stayed with him

for seven years. After the seven years were over he had said all that he had to say, for his conversation was limited, and he decided to return to his own castle. When he arrived he saw the children playing in the garden.

"What are you doing here?" he cried in a very gruff voice, and the children ran away.

"My own garden is my own garden," said the Giant; "anyone can understand that, and I will allow nobody to play in it but myself." So he built a high wall all round it and put up a notice-board.

> TRESPASSERS
> WILL BE
> PROSECUTED

He was a very selfish Giant.

The poor children had now nowhere to play. They tried to play on the road, but the road was very dusty and full of hard stones, and they did not like it. They used to wander round the high wall when their lessons were over and talk about the beautiful garden inside. "How happy we were there!" they said to each other.

Then the Spring came, and all over the country there were little blossoms and little birds. Only in the garden of the Selfish Giant it was still winter. The birds did not care to sing in it as there were no children, and the trees forgot to blossom. Once a beautiful flower put its head out from the grass, but when it saw the notice-board it was so sorry for the children that it slipped back into the ground again and went off to sleep.

    The only people who were pleased were the Snow and the Frost. "Spring has forgotten this garden," they cried, "so we will live here all the year round." The Snow covered up the grass with her great white cloak, and the Frost painted all the trees silver. Then they invited the North Wind to stay with them, and he came. He was wrapped in furs, and he roared all day about the garden, and blew the chimney-pots down. "This is a delightful spot," he said, "we must ask the Hail on a visit." So the Hail came. Every day for three hours he rattled on the roof of the castle till he broke most of the slates, and then he ran round and round the garden as fast as he could go. He was dressed in gray, and his breath was like ice.

    "I cannot understand why the Spring is so late in coming," said the Selfish Giant, as he sat at the window and looked out at his cold, white garden; "I hope there will be a change in the weather."

    But the Spring never came, nor the Summer. The Autumn gave golden fruit to every garden, but to the Giant's garden she gave none. "He is too selfish," she said. So it was always Winter there, and the North Wind and the Hail, and the Frost, and the Snow danced about through the trees.

    One morning the Giant was lying awake in bed when he heard some lovely music. It sounded so sweet to his ears that he thought it must be the King's musicians passing by. It was really only a little linnet singing outside his window, but it was so long since he had heard a bird sing in his garden that it seemed to him to be the most beautiful music in the world. Then the Hail stopped dancing over his head, and the North Wind ceased roaring, and a delicious perfume came to him through the open casement.

"I believe the Spring has come at last," said the Giant; and he jumped out of bed and looked out.

What did he see?

He saw a most wonderful sight. Through a little hole in the wall the children had crept in, and they were sitting in the branches of the trees. In every tree that he could see there was a little child. And the trees were so glad to have the children back again that they had covered themselves with blossoms and were waving their arms gently above the children's heads. The birds were flying about and twittering with delight, and the flowers were looking up through the green grass and laughing. It was a lovely scene, only in one corner it was still Winter. It was the farthest corner of the garden, and in it was standing a little boy. He was so small that he could not reach up to the branches of the tree, and he was wandering all round it, crying bitterly. The poor tree was still quite covered with frost and snow, and the North Wind was blowing and roaring above it. "Climb up! little boy," said the Tree, and it bent its branches down as low as it could; but the boy was too tiny.

And the Giant's heart melted as he looked out. "How selfish I have been!" he said; "now I know why the Spring would not come here. I will put that poor little boy on the top of the tree, and then I will knock down the wall, and my garden shall be the children's playground for ever and ever." He was really very sorry for what he had done.

So he crept downstairs and opened the front door quite softly and went out into the garden. But when the children saw him they were so frightened that they all ran away, and the garden became Winter again. Only the little boy did not run, for his eyes were so full of tears that he did not see the Giant coming. And the Giant stole up behind him and took him gently in his hand and put him up into the tree. And the tree broke at once into blossom, and the birds came and sang in it, and the little boy stretched out his two arms and flung them around the Giant's neck and kissed him. And the other children, when they saw that the Giant was not wicked any longer, came running back, and with them came the Spring.

"It is your garden now, little children," said the Giant, and he took a great ax and knocked down the wall. And when the people were going to market at twelve o'clock they found the Giant playing with the children in the most beautiful garden they had ever seen.

All day long they played, and in the evening they came to the Giant to bid him good-by.

"But where is your little companion?" he said, "the boy I put into the tree?" The Giant loved him the best because he had kissed him.

"We don't know," answered the children; "he has gone away."

"You must tell him to be sure and come here tomorrow," said the Giant. But the children said that they did not know where he lived, and had never seen him before; and the Giant felt very sad.

Every afternoon, when school was over, the children came and played with the Giant. But the little boy whom the Giant loved was never seen again. The Giant was very kind to all the children, yet he longed for his first little friend, and often spoke of him. "How I would like to see him!" he used to say.

Years went over, and the Giant grew very old and feeble. He could not play about any more, so he sat in a huge armchair and watched the children at their games, and admired his garden. "I have many beautiful flowers," he said; "but the children are the most beautiful flowers of all."

One winter morning he looked out of his window as he was dressing. He did not hate the Winter now, for he knew that it was merely the Spring asleep and that the flowers were resting.

Suddenly he rubbed his eyes in wonder and looked and looked. It certainly was a marvelous sight. In the farthest corner of the garden was a tree quite covered with lovely white blossoms. Its branches were all

golden, and silver fruit hung down from them, and underneath it stood the little boy he had loved.

Downstairs ran the Giant in great joy and out into the garden. He hastened across the grass and came near to the child. And when he came quite close his face grew red with anger, and he said, "Who hath dared to wound thee?" For on the palms of the child's hands were the prints of two nails, and the prints of two nails were on the little feet.

"Who hath dared to wound thee?" cried the Giant; "tell me, that I might take my big sword and slay him."

"Nay!" answered the child; "but these are the wounds of Love."

"Who art thou?" said the Giant, and a strange awe fell on him, and he knelt before the little child.

And the child smiled on the Giant, and said to him, "You let me play once in your garden, today you shall come with me to my garden, which is Paradise."

And when the children ran in that afternoon, they found the Giant lying dead under the tree, all covered with white blossoms.

There is deep devotion among Mexicans to the Blessed Mother, the Virgin of Guadalupe. Solemn pilgrimages are made to her shrine and, through the years, Mexicans have told the story of

Our Lady and the Aztec

JOSEPHINE M. O'NEIL

Once, when the New World was very new, there lived in a little Mexican village a lonely Aztec whose name was Juan Diego. Even his rough adobe hut was built far away from the dwellings of the other Indians. Juan's good wife, Maria Lucia, had died. He had no children. He seldom talked to anyone. The only person he ever visited was his uncle, Juan Bernardino, whom he loved very much. Years before, when Juan Diego was a boy, his father had died, and Juan Bernardino had taken care of him as if he were his own son. This uncle was a very old man now and lived in a stone house at the other end of town.

At dusk, when the merry sounds of laughter and song came from the distant houses of the village, Juan Diego would sit all alone near his own doorway. Never a word did he speak, for there was no one to listen. No song came from his lips, for there was no one in all the countryside to hear it.

Sometimes as he sat in silence at sundown, he would gaze upon his poor, neglected farm. The crooked rows of vegetables were overrun with weeds. Every kind of hungry insect ate up his corn and beans before they even had time to ripen. Greedy little birds and large screaming crows pecked away the fruit in his small orchard. All in all, Juan Diego was a poor farmer. But since he had no one with whom to share his corn and beans and bright red peppers, what did it matter? He himself needed very little to keep body and soul together.

The days from Monday until Friday were just alike to Juan Diego—silent, sad, and lonely. On Saturday, however, and on Sunday, he was a different person. When he thought of Saturday and Sunday, he would smile as if he had some happy secret unknown to others. The reason was that on those days, long before dawn, he made his way to the Chapel of Saint James, eight miles away over the hills. There the brown-robed Franciscan Father would be waiting for him and would call him by name. There he would take his place among the other Aztecs from near-by villages.

First they would hear Mass. When it was over, the Father would talk to them as if they were his children. He would tell them about heaven, where perhaps good Maria Lucia was already enjoying the happy company of angels and saints. He would tell them about God the Father, who made us all, and the Son of God, who became man and lived on earth to teach us and to give up His life for us. And then the priest would speak of Mary, Our Lord's Holy Mother, and of Saint Joseph, the humble carpenter of Nazareth.

Juan Diego treasured the priest's words. Again and again on his way home he would think of them. And in the lonely hours as he sat by the door of his hut, everything the brown-robed Father had taught them would come back to him.

Every Saturday morning saw the little Aztec plodding over the sharp rocks and clumps of cactus in the direction of the village where the small mission chapel stood. Every Saturday he went and returned in much the same manner. But one Saturday was different. And that day changed the course of Juan Diego's whole life.

It was the ninth of December. The week before, the priest had told the Indians all about Our Blessed Lady's Immaculate Conception. Today, the second of the eight days that would be devoted to celebrating that great feast, they were to hear Our Lady's Mass and afterward the Father would tell them more about her.

When Juan set out, the air was chill and the morning still dark. He scarcely noticed how sharp the rough stones were, or how prickly the cactus was, beneath his poorly shod feet. Eagerly he hurried along, for he wanted to be in his place when the priest called his name.

He soon reached the top of a high hill. Suddenly, as if from nowhere, the strangest, sweetest music filled the air all about him. It was like a melody made up of the most delightful bird notes ever heard. Juan looked around, but saw nothing unusual. No band of wandering musicians approached from the other side of the mountain. Not a single bird hovered in the crisp December air. Yet the sound still continued.

So charmed was the little Aztec by the glorious sweetness of the music that he asked himself, "Have I died and gone to heaven?" He climbed to the very peak of the mountain, and there he saw a cloud which seemed to have caught all the fairest colors of sunrise. Such a light was shining from its center that he could barely look at it. Then he heard a voice from the cloud calling him by name.

"Juan Diego, Juan Diego," it said in the Aztec language, "my own dearly loved child, where are you going so early in the morning?"

Looking up, Juan saw a most beautiful Lady. She

wore a sky-blue veil and mantle, and her dress was the color of roses, with delicate flowers embroidered on it. The light of the sunrise-cloud surrounding her shone on the stones at her feet and made them glitter like jewels; it struck the leaves of the little stunted trees and made them look like radiant emeralds; even the bare, rough ground gleamed as if it were polished gold.

The Lady's voice was so gentle and so loving that the timid little Aztec was not afraid. He replied to her question at once, "Most honored one, I am on my way to the Chapel of Saint James. There I shall hear Mass and listen to the good Father who teaches the Indians the truths of heaven."

"Juan Diego, my good and faithful son, know that I am Mary Ever-Virgin, Mother of the True God, the Creator of all things, the Lord of heaven and earth. For you I have a very special errand."

Kneeling, the Indian replied, "Most honored Mother in heaven and on earth, I will do whatever it is your pleasure to ask."

"Go then, my son, to the Bishop of Mexico City. Tell him it is my wish that in my honor there be built in this place a chapel. I am the Mother of all your people, and here I will show my love and compassion for them, and for all who seek my aid. Here I will comfort those who are sorrowful, and be with those whose trials are greatest. Tell the Bishop this is my request. Tell him, my son, all that you have seen and heard."

As if he had always been a courtier in the service of a queen, the humble little Aztec bowed graciously.

"Most honored one," he said, "I am your lowly servant. Speedily will I do what you ask." Then, rising, he hastened in the direction of Mexico City.

All the sadness and loneliness were gone from Juan Diego's heart. Joyfully he went on his way, wondering if in the whole world a messenger had ever carried so precious a secret.

Madonna Remembers

SISTER M. EDWARDINE, R.S.M.

Madonna loves
The first white buds of May
That little children bring
To lay before her feet.
Madonna's heart sings
When they kneel
In briefest prayer,
Just for a moment snatched
From marbles and kites and ball.
She would gather up
Giver and gift,
Holding them tight
Within her mantle's blue,
For then
Madonna sees again
An old, forgotten garden
Where a little Lad,
In Nazareth,
Left other boys and play
To bring for her delight
The first white buds of May.

Little Pear

ELEANOR FRANCES LATTIMORE

It was a hot day in the middle of the summer. The sun blazed down on the village and on Little Pear, who was strolling along the street, eating a cucumber. His bare feet shuffled through the thick yellow dust. "Ay-ah," he sighed, "how hot it is!—and where are all my friends?"

The street was deserted, and the reason was that nearly everyone was asleep. It was too hot for most people to want to walk about. It was even too hot for the children to want to play. Little Pear, though, always wanted to be doing something. "I know what I shall do," he thought. "I shall go and watch the boats on the river." Just then he saw a child trotting around the corner. He felt quite excited for a minute, because he had walked nearly through half the village and had seen only a pig and a few chickens. But when the child came nearer he saw that it was only Big Head's baby brother.

The baby was dressed in a little red apron shaped like a diamond. It was all that he had on, because Chinese babies don't wear very much in the summer. His head was shaved except for a fringe of hair across his forehead. He was trotting along in a great hurry until he met Little Pear, who stopped him. "You must not run away," said Little Pear, and he took the baby's hand and led him back to the home of Big Head, who was leaning against the doorway, fast asleep. Little Pear lifted the little brother over the doorstep and gave him the rest of his cucumber. "Stay where you are," he said. "You might get lost if you run away." Then he had a good idea. He took the good-luck chain off his own neck and put it around the baby's. "Now you will be safe," he said, and he patted the baby kindly on the head and strolled on, feeling very good. Again he thought, "I shall go to the river and watch the ships," and he started off in the direction of the river.

It was a long way to the river. Little Pear followed the path that cut across the fields and soon left the village far behind him. The sun blazed down on Little Pear as he pattered along in his bare feet. The fields were as deserted as the village. There was no sound except for the singing of locusts in the willow trees as he drew near the river.

Presently he stood on the high bank, looking down

at the river. First he looked up the river, and then he looked down the river; and all the time he remembered to hold tight to a willow tree with both hands.

The river was swift and muddy. The sun shining on it made the ripples first brown and then blue. The bank opposite Little Pear, like the bank that he was standing on, was bordered by rough-barked willow trees leaning out over the water. Between the banks the boats went busily up and down. Here everybody seemed to be very wide-awake. Little Pear thought of the sleepy village he had left and was glad that he had come to the river.

There were all kinds of boats. Big boats with masts and sails and smaller boats with none, and boats with great fishing-nets spread out like huge spiderwebs. There were flat boats, too, laden with things to sell. Some had cabbages, and some had rolls of matting, and some had bags that might be filled with all sorts of interesting things, Little Pear thought.

The big boats had eyes painted on them in front, so that they could see where they were going. The owners of these boats were careful not to let anything hang over the edge in front of the eyes, for then the boats could not have seen their way as they sailed in and out among the smaller boats.

Little Pear wished that he had a boat of his own, but he couldn't decide whether he would rather have a small one that he could row, or a larger one that he could push with a pole, or a big one with a sail.

Finally Little Pear decided that what he would like most of all to have when he grew up would be a fishing-boat. For then he could catch fish for his meals and take fish to the city to sell, and what fun that would be!

Little Pear held tight to the willow tree and gazed at the ships going up and down. He was wishing that he would grow up soon, when suddenly he saw, drawing nearer and nearer, the loveliest kind of boat on the river. It was a houseboat!

"That is the kind of boat I should like to have," thought Little Pear, as he watched it drawing nearer and nearer. It was a long flat boat with a real little house on it, with a hole in the ceiling for the smoke to go through, and paper windows. A man was walking up and down the side of the deck, shoving with a long pole.

Little Pear looked admiringly at the clothes hanging out to dry and watched the children playing about the deck, and the boat sailed gaily along until it was quite close to Little Pear.

Suddenly one of the children saw him. He called to his brothers and sisters, and they all flocked to the edge of the boat and waved to Little Pear as he stood alone on the bank. It made him feel very happy and, without thinking, he let go of his tree to wave back. *Slip*, went his feet on the steep bank—slip, slide—and *plop*, into the river fell Little Pear!

The brown water whirled round and round him in circles as he rose to the surface, choking and sputtering. "Ay-ah!" cried the children on the boat. "He is drowning, he is drowning!" For Little Pear could not swim, and the swift current was carrying him away from the bank. He splashed around wildly with his arms and was about to sink again when the man on the boat rushed forward and reached out his pole. "Catch hold!" he cried.

Little Pear couldn't hear what the man said, for there was water in his ears. He could scarcely see the man, for there was water in his eyes! He couldn't say anything himself, for he had swallowed so much water—but he splashed around with his arms—and—he caught hold of the pole! Then he held on tight while the man pulled him to the side of the boat and lifted him safely to the deck.

For some time he lay there, wondering to himself whether he was drowned or not, and thinking that perhaps he would never see his family again. Then he opened his eyes and saw above him a circle of faces. Here he was on the houseboat, and here were the children who had waved to him and the man who had saved him. There was the kindly face of the mother, too, who had hurried out of the little house to see what had happened.

Little Pear smiled at them, and they all exclaimed over him, saying what a wonder it was that he wasn't drowned; and they admired his flowered jacket and the green string around his pigtail.

"Will you stay with us?" asked the children.

But their mother said, "No, this little boy comes from the shore, and his family will wonder where he is. He must go home when we come to the next landing-place."

The boat sailed on down the river. Little Pear sat drying in the sun, while the children sat around him in a circle, telling him about their life on the river, and asking him eager questions about the land. "We have never lived on the land," they told him, "because this boat has always been our home."

Then Little Pear told them about his village and about his family and friends and his canary. As he talked he began to think how glad he would be to see them all again. But the boat sailed on down the busy river, taking Little Pear farther and farther away from home.

When they finally reached the next landing-place, the houseboat stopped and Little Pear was set ashore. He felt very sorry to say good-by to his new friends. He climbed the path up the bank and watched until the boat had sailed on, far down the river. The children were still waving to him, but Little Pear held tight to a tree with both hands, because he didn't want to fall into the water again. The boat disappeared around a bend in the river, and Little Pear started for home.

Away across the fields the sun was setting. Little Pear walked on, and on, and on. The way home was long, as the boat had sailed a mile or two down the river. "Ay-ah," thought Little Pear, "soon it will be dark!" And he hurried his tired feet along more quickly. The path along the river bank was deserted, the fields were deserted, and it seemed as though in all the world there was nobody except Little Pear.

Little Pear walked on, and on, and on. The sun had been down for a long time, and the night was very dark, when at last Little Pear saw ahead of him the dim outline of the village. Dogs barked at him as he approached. "Don't bark!" he cried. "Don't you know me? This is Little Pear!" When he reached his own gateway the stone lions on either side of it looked very fierce. "They are roaring now, not laughing," he thought, and he said aloud, "Don't bite me. This is Little Pear!" He ran across the courtyard to the house. "Open the door!" he cried. "It is Little Pear!"

Then the door was flung open, and "It is Little Pear!" cried his mother and Dagu and Ergu all at once, throwing their arms around him.

How glad Little Pear was to be at home again! And how glad his family were to see him! "Where have you been?" they cried. "We have hunted for you all afternoon, and the men are still out with lanterns, looking for you."

Little Pear told them all that had happened, how he had left the village and had gone to the river, and how he had fallen into the river and been rescued. Then his mother prepared some hot food for him while Dagu put the kettle on to boil and Ergu sped away to tell all the village that Little Pear had returned.

Soon there was the sound of many feet in the courtyard, and then the tiny room was filled with people. There were Little Pear's father and the other men who had been searching with him for Little Pear. There was Ergu, out of breath and with shining eyes. There were all the nearest neighbors and best friends. There was Big Head, looking very excited, and Big Head's baby brother. He still had the good-luck chain around his neck.

"You may keep the chain," Little Pear told him, "for you are very little and something might happen to you. But I am a big boy, and I am never going to run away again."

Then everybody was very happy. They patted Little Pear on the head. "We all loved you very much when you were naughty," they said, "but we shall love you even more if you are good."

"I will always be a good boy, now," Little Pear promised, nodding his head very hard. Ergu looked at her small brother and suddenly felt rather sad.

"Little Pear is growing up," she said.

Saint of the Sea

Beyond the orchards,
beyond the tangled grapevines,
past the gray-green branches
of twisted olive trees,
Galilee dips down to the sea.

The waves lap the shore,
the shore of golden sand
where the fishing boats,
the dark, wet boats
of the fishermen of Galilee,
drift in silver fog.

The summer comes,
the summer goes
in Galilee.
So it is today;
so it was in that holy yesterday
when the message of God went forth
that His only begotten Son had come
to save the souls of men.

Men in the fields of Galilee
heard the message of God,
but they did not believe,
though the Son of God
walked among them, telling them,
"The Kingdom of God is at hand."

Past the roads and the green fields,
past the orchards and the olive trees,
Christ came to the shore of the inland sea,
to the boat of Peter the fisherman.
There, as Peter cast his net into the waters,
the Son of God said to him,
"Come, follow Me, and I will
make you a fisher of men."

Though Peter knew
that the footsteps of Jesus Christ
would lead to a lonely hill,
and to sorrow and death,
he was not afraid.
He believed, and his heart
was filled with joy.

He left his boat,
he left his fishing nets,
he left his quiet home
and followed the Son of God
to Judea, to Jerusalem,
to the dark heights of Calvary;
for, beyond the darkness,
beyond the torment and the tears,
Peter the Apostle knew
that Jesus Christ would lead him
to everlasting life.

The Barefoot Boy

JOHN GREENLEAF WHITTIER

Blessings on thee, little man,
Barefoot boy, with cheek of tan!
With thy turned-up pantaloons,
And thy merry whistled tunes;
With thy red lip, redder still
Kissed by strawberries on the hill;
With the sunshine on thy face,
Through thy torn brim's jaunty grace;
From my heart I give thee joy,—
I was once a barefoot boy!
Prince thou art,—the grown-up man
Only is republican.
Let the million-dollared ride!
Barefoot, trudging at his side,
Thou hast more than he can buy
In the reach of ear and eye,—
Outward sunshine, inward joy:
Blessings on thee, barefoot boy!

Oh for boyhood's painless play,
Sleep that wakes in laughing day,
Health that mocks the doctor's rules,
Knowledge never learned of schools,
Of the wild bee's morning chase,
Of the wild-flower's time and place,
Flight of fowl and habitude
Of the tenants of the wood,

How the tortoise bears his shell,
How the woodchuck digs his cell,
And the ground-mole sinks his well;
How the robin feeds her young,
How the oriole's nest is hung;
Where the whitest lilies blow,
Where the freshest berries grow,
Where the ground-nut trails its vine,
Where the wood-grape's clusters shine;
Of the black wasp's cunning way,
Mason of his walls of clay,
And the architectural plans
Of gray hornet artisans!
For, eschewing books and tasks,
Nature answers all he asks;
Hand in hand with her he walks,
Face to face with her he talks,
Part and parcel of her joy,—
Blessings on the barefoot boy!

Oh for boyhood's time of June,
Crowding years in one brief moon,
When all things I heard or saw,
Me, their master, waited for.
I was rich in flowers and trees,
Humming-birds and honey-bees;
For my sport the squirrel played,
Plied the snouted mole his spade;
For my taste the blackberry cone
Purpled over hedge and stone;
Laughed the brook for my delight
Through the day and through the night,
Whispering at the garden wall,
Talked with me from fall to fall;
Mine the sand-rimmed pickerel pond,
Mine the walnut slopes beyond,
Mine, on bending orchard trees,
Apples of Hesperides!
Still as my horizon grew,
Larger grew my riches too;
All the world I saw or knew
Seemed a complex Chinese toy,
Fashioned for a barefoot boy!
Oh for festal dainties spread,
Like my bowl of milk and bread;
Pewter spoon and bowl of wood,
On the door-stone gray and rude!
O'er me, like a regal tent,
Cloudy-ribbed, the sunset bent,

Purple-curtained, fringed with gold,
Looped in many a wind-swung fold:
While for music came the play
Of the pied frogs' orchestra;
And, to light the noisy choir,
Lit the fly his lamp of fire.
I was monarch: pomp and joy
Waited on the barefoot boy!

Cheerily, then, my little man,
Live and laugh, as boyhood can!
Though the flinty slopes be hard,
Stubble-speared the new-mown sward,
Every morn shall lead thee through
Fresh baptisms of the dew;
Every evening from thy feet
Shall the cool wind kiss the heat:
All too soon these feet must hide
In the prison cells of pride,
Lose the freedom of the sod,
Like a colt's for work be shod,
Made to tread the mills of toil,
Up and down in ceaseless moil:
Happy if their track be found
Never on forbidden ground;
Happy if they sink not in
Quick and treacherous sands of sin.
Ah, that thou couldst know thy joy,
Ere it passes, barefoot boy!

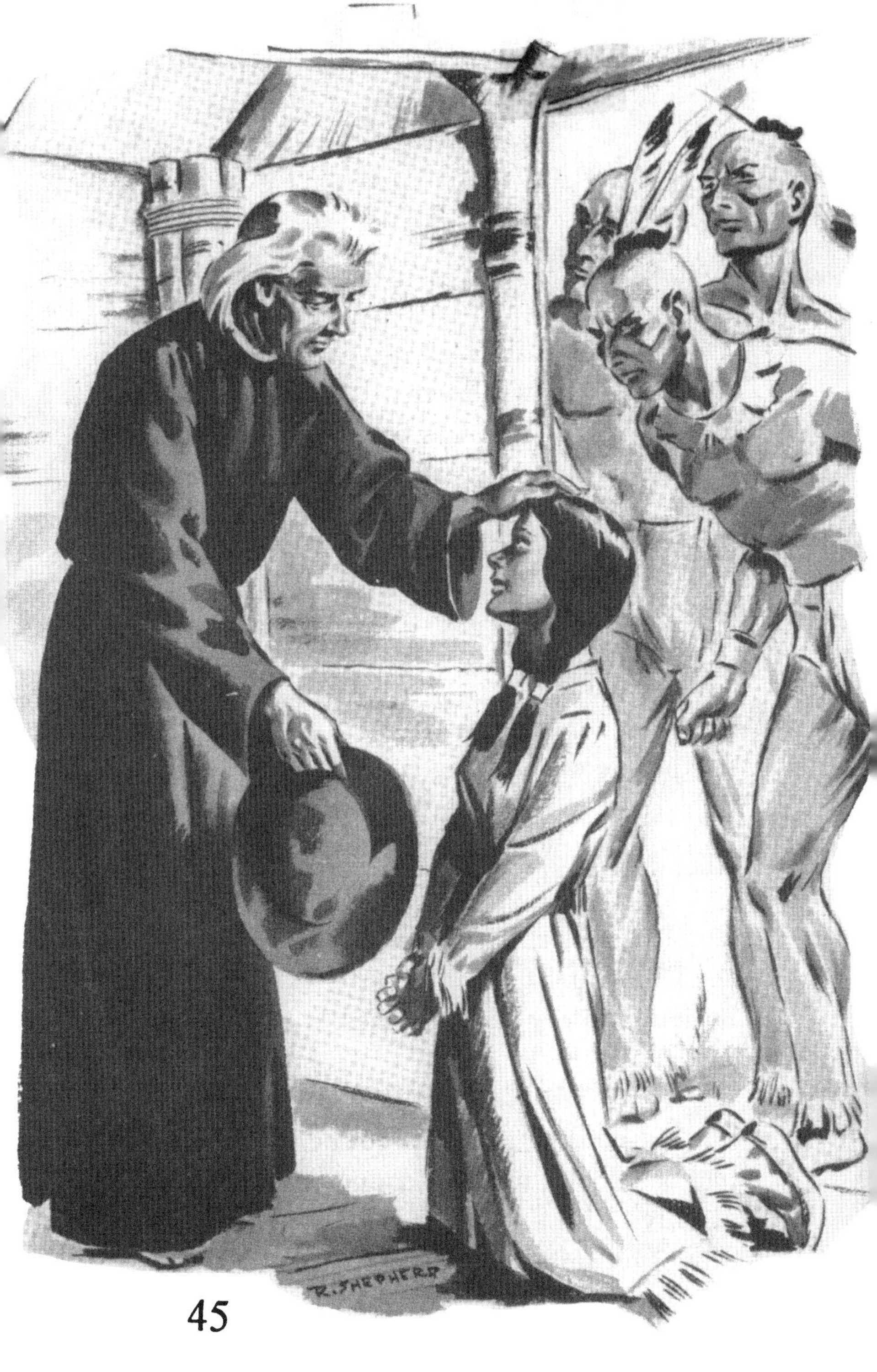
R. SHEPHERD

Lily of the Mohawks

Between the Hudson
and Lake Erie,
from east to west,
stretched the country of the Mohawks.
There, where Lake George and Lake Champlain
meet the Mohawk River,
Kateri Tekakwitha was born,
in a cabin built of great branches
where screens of wild fur skins hung
as shelter from the wind.

A shy little Indian girl,
she dwelt among her tribe
of fierce and hardened warriors.
They called themselves
"the people of the Long House."
They knew how to use the arrow.
They knew how to use firearms.

Her father, a chief, fought
the Dutch and the French;
he fought other Indian tribes:
the Hurons,
the Algonquins;
but her mother, an Algonquin captive,
had been born, instructed, and baptized
at Three Rivers, in Quebec.
She never forgot her Faith.

After her father died,
after her mother died
she lived in the house
of her uncle, near a little river.
She pounded Indian corn.
She carried water from a little spring
that, to this day, is called
"Tekakwitha's Spring."
She brought in the firewood.
She hunted the forest for small game,
for berries, for honey, for nuts.
She made beaded moccasins,
tobacco bags for the warriors,
leggings for the hunters,
bark cradles for Indian babies.
On a rosary made of kernels of corn
she repeated the prayers
her mother had taught her.

Missionaries came to the long house
and to the village beyond.
They stayed a little while.
They taught Kateri Tekakwitha.
They baptized her one Easter morning
in a little chapel
bright with boughs
and spring flowers.

When the black-robed priests were gone
on their heroic mission,
the Mohawks taunted Kateri Tekakwitha.
They jeered at her.
They mocked her.
They hurled stones at her.
They would have put her to death
for her Faith.

A brave Christian Indian saved her.
He urged her to join a forlorn little company
bound for Canada.
They followed the Mohawk River
on its bend to the east.
Through vast forests they moved,
through thickets and bushes,
among trees covered with vines,
until they came at last
to the Canadian mission.

There Kateri Tekakwitha was safe.
There, with the gift of Faith
as a strong shield
against old fears,
she lived and died
in holiness,
in kindness,
in charity.

No Canadian writer loved his native land more than Bliss Carman.
He voiced some of his appreciation of these northern provinces
in the poem

Trees

BLISS CARMAN

In the Garden of Eden, planted by God,
There were goodly trees in the springing sod,—

Trees of beauty and height and grace,
To stand in splendor before his face.

Apple and hickory, ash and pear,
Oak and beech and the tulip rare,

The trembling aspen, the noble pine,
The sweeping elm by the river line;

Trees for the birds to build and sing,
And the lilac tree for a joy in spring;

Trees to turn at the frosty call
And carpet the ground for the Lord's footfall;

Trees for fruitage and fire and shade,
Trees for the cunning builder's trade;

He made them of every grain and girth,
For the use of man in the Garden of Earth.

Then lest the soul should not lift her eyes
From the gift to the Giver of Paradise,

On the crown of a hill, for all to see,
God planted a scarlet maple tree.

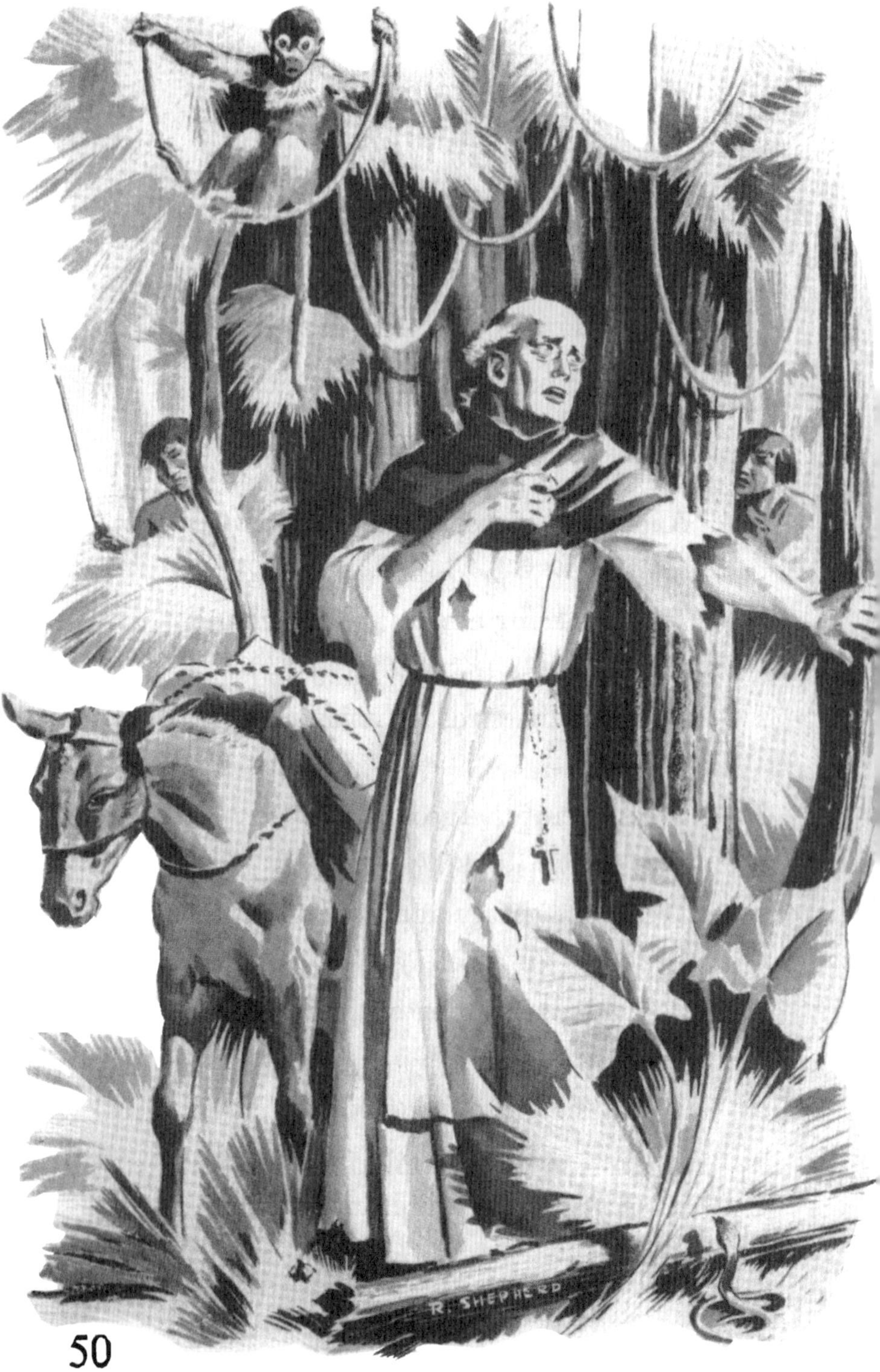
R. SHEPHERD

Apostle of South America

Did you ever hear the story of Louis Bertrand?
If you lived below the Rio Grande River,
in the islands of the West Indies,
you would know his name,
you would know his story.

For Louis Bertrand,
gentle, quiet, saintly Louis Bertrand,
friar preacher, priest, and missionary
has been long remembered
in the lands below the border.
Out of Spain, out of the soft beauty of Valencia,
Louis Bertrand crossed the stormy sea to become
the Apostle of South America.

He loved the quiet gardens of Valencia,
and the blue waters of the Mediterranean
that stretched below the house of his father.
He loved the learned ways of Valencia,
books, music, old portraits on old walls,
portraits of Spanish noblemen,
portraits of Spanish ladies,
the rich, glowing likeness of the saint of the family,
Saint Vincent Ferrer, who had left the court of kings
to walk among the lowly.

But beyond Valencia, far beyond,
across the wide Atlantic,
was the New Spain.

Christopher Columbus had sailed
out from a Spanish port
to find it.
Cortez, Spanish adventurer, had sailed to the west.
Pizarro, with armies of the Spanish king, had followed
   him.
Some men, greedy for gold, had sailed
to the new land.

Louis Bertrand, in the quiet of Valencia,
dreamed of the mission work.
"There," he sighed, "the fields are white,
white for the harvest of souls."
When the Dominican call came for volunteers
for the mission fields,
Louis Bertrand answered the call.

The lands below the Rio Grande, the hot, wet lands,
were wild lands.
Monkeys screamed from matted branches,
jaguars, their sleek coats bright as sunlight,
leaped stealthily, softly, from overhanging boughs.
High mountains blocked the way of Louis Bertrand.
Dank marshes slowed his footsteps.
Pagan Indians poisoned him
and, for days, he lay near death.
Hunger stalked him.
Loneliness assailed him.

In the valleys of the Magdalena,
through wet grass and under tall coconut palm,
Louis Bertrand walked alone.
He had an armor of faith.
His weapon was his lifted hand, his slim, white hand,
with which he made the Sign of the Cross.

Indians, who had come to slay, remained to watch him.
They watched and wondered.
Then they stayed near the white-robed stranger
until he taught them the rosary,
until he baptized them,
until he blessed them once more
with the Sign of the Cross
and moved to the tribe beyond.

In seven years he baptized thousands of Indians,
in the province of Saint Martha,
in the Leeward Islands,
in Saint Vincent and Saint Thomas,
and from Panama to Cartagena.

Louis Bertrand, Saint of God, left behind him
a beautiful land,
made more beautiful
by his service to man.
He left behind him a grateful people,
who had been given the grace of God
by a brave gesture
of his slim white hand.

Chi-weé's mother could not make pottery to sell unless she found a certain kind of clay. That is what led to the adventure of

Chi-weé and the Rabbit

GRACE PURDIE MOON

Chi-weé was not her real name. She had a long Indian one, very hard to pronounce, but she was so little and so fat that a long, thin name didn't suit her at all. So, once, when she was a wee roly-poly baby, she had tried to imitate a little bird who sang for her and the sound she made was so like "chee-wee" that she had been called by that name ever since!

Chi-weé lived alone with her mother in one room of a stone house in the pueblo, and they were very poor. Her mother made pottery jars to sell to their neighbors and to the white people who came often to the hill, which is called a mesa. The jars were very strong and beautifully shaped—no one in all the Indian pueblos could make prettier jars, or finer designs on them—but they were all dull brown and black in color, and it seemed that everyone wanted red jars. The Indian trader at the canyon store had told her, "If you will bring me red jars as well made as these brown ones, I will take all you can bring and pay you well."

So Chi-weé had heard her mother often say, "If only we could find the red clay—surely others have found it or there would be no red jars—but nowhere in all our land have I seen the red clay."

And so they remained poor, and Chi-weé would go to the trader's store and look longingly at the jars of red-and-white striped candy that he had so temptingly spread out on his shelves, and at the great rolls of wonderful cloth that would make such beautiful dresses for a little girl—but for some little girl whose mother had money with which to buy—and a big, hard lump would come in her throat at the thought. Once, her mother had told her, they had had all these things as other people had, but that was long before she could remember, when she had been a baby, and she had a father who worked in the fields with the other men and brought home rabbits and other game from the hunt. But he had gone away a long, long time ago, down the silent trail to the Lost Others, her mother said, and had never come back.

But today was a happy day in the pueblo, and for Chi-weé, sad, sad thoughts were never long in her mind, and today they had no place at all, for it was a gala day and there was to be a great dance in the afternoon. Chi-weé was not to take part in the dance, but it was such fun to watch the queer clowns and all the wonderful costumes of the dancers. There were the men who were painted white with streaks of black and who wore long fox tails dragging on the ground and rattles of sheep's hoofs about their ankles; and those who wore tall, wooden painted headdresses that looked like butterflies and birds; and the women with garlands of flowers and bunches of evergreens in their hands. And then, there were the good things to eat—little seed cakes and candies made with pinyon nuts for the children. And many white people came to the pueblo for the day—men, women, and even little children—and all the Indians were in their best and brightest clothes.

Chi-weé, too, was dressed in her very best—a pink calico waist with a brown skirt, and around her waist a woven belt of red and green with tassels hanging at the side. Her black hair hung loose about her shoulders and she wore a little black shawl—but best of all were her white boots that came clear up to her knees! Of those boots she was more proud than of anything else, and she and her mother had worked hard that morning with white clay to make them spotless and gleaming. No little girl in the pueblo had whiter boots than Chi-weé, and she was very sure that even the white visitors admired them, though, of course, white people knew very little about such things!

All the work of the little home had been done very early that morning—the floor was brushed clean and every basket and little jar and piece of clothing was in its place, and Chi-weé felt proud and happy that she could help her mother to keep it so fresh and clean. Now she could enjoy the whole day with no thoughts of work undone to bother her.

Some time before the dance was to begin, Chi-weé's mother called to her and, giving her a small water jar, told the little girl to go down the trail to the spring and bring back the jar full of water.

Usually the mother went herself, but today she did not feel strong. Chi-weé was frightened when she saw how pale her mother looked.

"It is nothing, little daughter," the mother said, when she saw the look in the little girl's eyes. "I should be strong if we had meat to eat. Ah, if we could only find the red clay—then we could have meat and many good things," and she sighed. "But go, Chi-weé, or you will be late for the dance."

So Chi-weé started down the trail with her water jar. She could not feel unhappy for long on such a wonderful day with the sun shining and all the world dressed up for a dance.

"Surely," she thought, "surely, the Good Spirit, who takes care of all the world, will take care of my mother too." And she forgot all about everything but just being happy.

The trail was steep, and she almost ran all the way

down, so it did not take her long to reach the spring, but she was warm and out of breath when she reached it and sat down on a big rock to rest.

How big the desert looked from here and how quiet after all the excitement of the mesa top! She could see far, far away to the sharp blue hills, and the queer-shaped rocks that looked like ships and great animals and high buildings against the horizon. But Chi-weé did not rest long; she filled her jar at the spring and, balancing it on her head, was just about to start up the trail again, when, suddenly, a little brown rabbit popped up from a big bunch of sagebrush just a few feet away, and Chi-weé was instantly all excitement. She felt that she could easily catch him by throwing her shawl over him and oh, how strong and fine her mother would feel if she could have a rabbit stew for supper!

She carefully lowered the jar from her head, not taking her eye from the rabbit; but her small shaking hands set it too suddenly on the rocks—BANG!—went the little pottery jar, smashed to bits! But she hardly looked at it, her eyes were still on the rabbit. Her mother would forgive her for the broken jar if only she could bring home the rabbit. It had bounded away at the sound of the breaking jar, but had stopped just a short distance farther on, to look back and see what had happened.

Chi-wee took her shawl in her hand and crept as carefully as she could toward the little animal. It saw her coming and went jumping away through the sage, the wee bit of tail looking very comical as it went up and down, up and down, with every jump. But this was a very curious little rabbit and instead of "hippity-hopping" clear out of sight, as most rabbits do, he would go just a short way and stop at a bush and look back at Chi-weé to see if she were still following. He seemed very friendly and at times Chi-weé almost wished he did not have to be made into a stew; but then she would think of her mother and run all the faster for the thought. Each time the rabbit stopped Chi-weé thought *surely* she would catch him and got her shawl all ready to throw over him, when—WHISK!—there he was off again to the next big bush!

The dance was altogether forgotten, and her mother, and her best clean clothes, and Chi-weé thought of nothing at all but that little brown rabbit and how she would *surely* catch him the next time he stopped.

On they went—and on—and on—over great patches of dry grass and sand, and places where rocks rolled under her feet and she slipped and slid and almost fell; places where the dry pinyon cones crackled under her feet and cactus thorns scratched her and tore her dress. Chi-weé grew hot and breathless, and the minutes slipped gradually into hours, but each time, now, it seemed as if the rabbit stopped for a longer while and she thought he *must* be getting tired, as she was. She would surely catch him *this* time!

They came to a little wash now, a place that had been a stream just a short while ago, in the rainy season. The little rabbit went down one bank of this and up the other side. Then came more sagebrush and rocks and desert—and then another wash! The rabbit ran straight up this one, and Chi-weé came to places that were still wet from the rains—one place was *splashy!*—and another—another! And she stopped suddenly as she realized that her lovely white boots, her dress, and even her hands and face were streaked and splashed with mud!

Her little heart sank within her and she forgot the rabbit, whose wee bit of tail bobbed out of sight, this time without being followed or noticed at all. Oh! what would her mother say? And the dance?—why, it was getting late, the sun was low—perhaps the dance was over! Oh, *why* had she been so foolish?—and she hadn't even caught the little rabbit after all—and she had broken the water jar!

Chi-weé felt that this was the very saddest day in all her life—this day that had begun so beautifully—and her heart was almost breaking. She turned around and started slowly for home.

There was the place where she had splashed through the mud—and there was more—the sticky stuff filled the whole wash, and Chi-weé had to climb the bank to avoid going through it again. And, oh, what a sight her boots were!

She started to run now and ran as fast as she could the long, long way back to the foot of the mesa where the trail came down to the spring. The tears were pouring down her cheeks, but she didn't care—it seemed as if nothing much mattered any more.

It was almost dark when Chi-weé reached home and she felt, at first, as if she could not go in; but then she slowly pushed open the door and walked into the little room.

A delicious odor floated out of the door as she opened it, and her mother was bending over a little fire of glowing coals stirring something in an iron pot. It was from the iron pot that the delicious odor came. The mother spoke quietly, without turning her head, "Where have you been, little daughter?"

Chi-weé did not answer, the cry lump in her throat was too big and hard and her eyes grew blind with fresh tears.

Her mother turned around then and her own eyes grew large and strange as she looked at the little girl.

"It—it—it—was a little rabbit," sobbed Chi-weé. "I wanted it for—y-o-u—my mother—oh, I wanted it so!" and the little voice went off into wails of grief.

Her mother rose slowly and came toward the little girl; then she knelt down and looked at the splashed boots. Suddenly her hands began to tremble and she scraped off a bit of the mud with her finger and examined it carefully.

"Where have you been, Chi-weé?" she asked, excitedly, then. "Tell me, where have you been?"

This was very different from what she had expected, and Chi-weé felt the sobs stop in her throat. Her hands came down from her eyes and she looked at her mother in wonder. There were bright-red spots in the cheeks that had been so pale, and she almost shook the little girl in her excitement.

"Over there," pointed Chi-weé, " 'way over there. The mud was in a wash—"

"Is there more of this same mud?" questioned her mother. "Very much more of this same mud?"

"Oh, yes," said Chi-weé, "and it is very sticky—there is enough to make a whole town."

"Oh, my daughter," said the mother then, kneeling down by the little girl and putting her arms about her, "do not cry, this is a very happy day for us."

Chi-weé opened her eyes wider yet. What strange things were happening! She had thought it was a very sad day—just a moment before she had thought that. What *could* her mother mean?

"See," said the mother again, "it is the red clay you have found—the red clay for which we have looked so long. And now I will make many jars that the trader will buy and, oh, little one, we shall have *many* things. And the dance will not be until tomorrow, for Che-day, who leads the dance, could not come today. And see, what the teacher lady brought—for me, a rabbit—I have made it into a beautiful stew for our supper; and for you—look on the little stone in the corner."

And following the pointing finger, Chi-weé saw, on the little stone that was her own, a jar—a wonderful jar, of the kind the trader kept on his shelves—a jar filled with the red-and-white striped candy of her dreams!

An Indian Summer Day on the Prairie

VACHEL LINDSAY

In the Beginning

The sun is a huntress young,
The sun is a red, red joy,
The sun is an Indian girl,
Of the tribe of the Illinois.

Mid-morning

The sun is a smoldering fire,
That creeps through the high gray plain,
And leaves not a bush of cloud
To blossom with flowers of rain.

Noon

The sun is a wounded deer,
That treads pale grass in the skies,
Shaking his golden horns,
Flashing his baleful eyes.

Sunset

The sun is an eagle old,
There in the windless west,
Atop of the spirit-cliffs
He builds him a crimson nest.

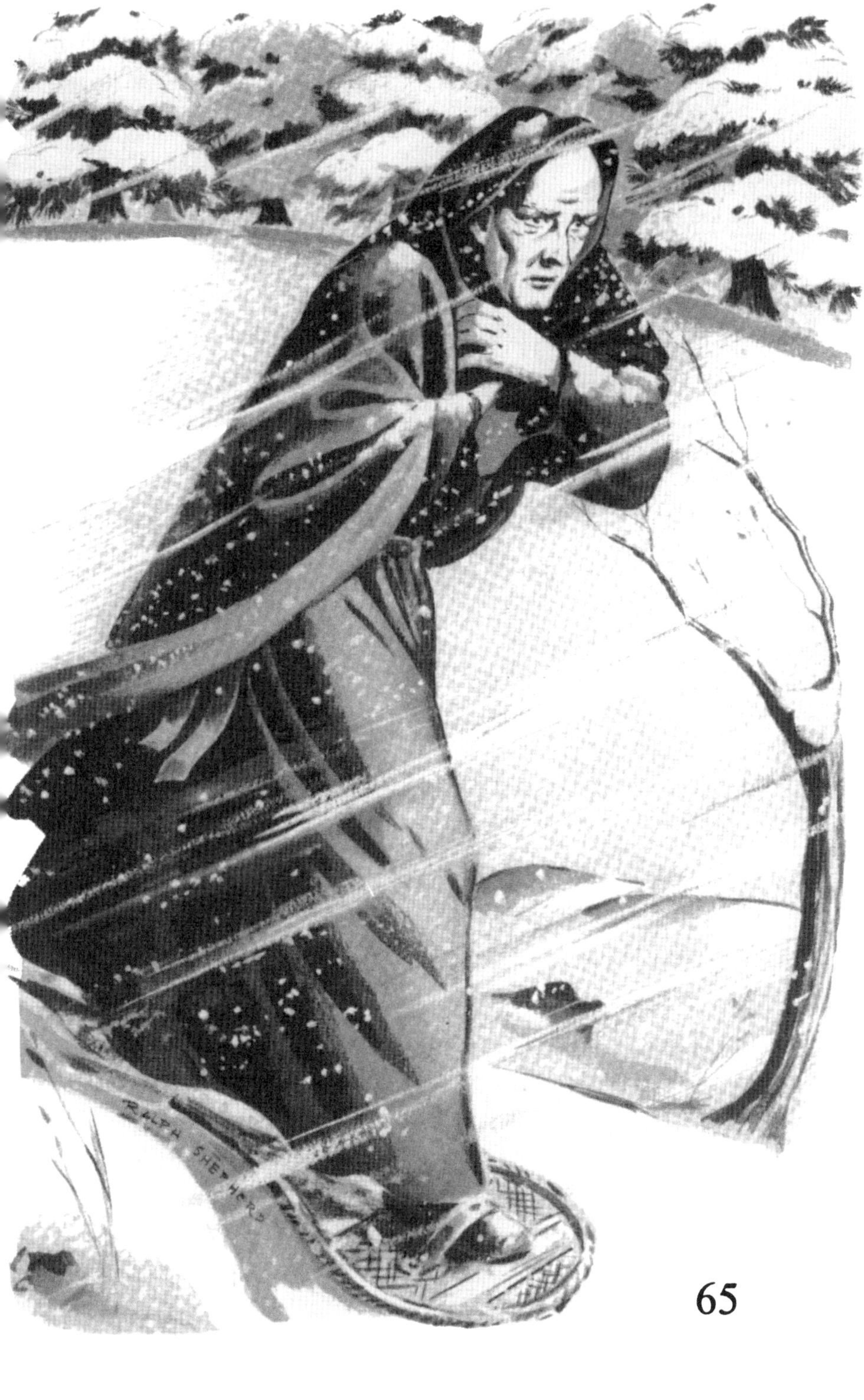
RALPH SHEPHERD

Apostle of the North

In winter now,
when the wind whistles down the River St. Lawrence,
when wolves howl in the lonely stretches of the Canadian north
far beyond its bright cities and gay villages,
the little children of Quebec
gather in the gleam of firelight
and listen to the story of the good Father Pierre,
a Jesuit who died in an act of kindness
long, long ago,
when Canada was young.

Father Pierre, old, humble, dutiful, kind,
set out from a settlement at Three Rivers
on a January night,
a night when northern lights flared above
the frozen river,
to go to a fort built by the French,
at the mouth of another river,
eighteen miles away.

His highway was the River St. Lawrence,
then a lane of solid ice,
buried, like all the northern land,
beneath a blanket of snow.
Before night Father Pierre had walked miles and miles,
and he was tired, and rested.

Before dawn, the cold dawn of the north,
the weather changed.
The air thickened,
clouds hid the moon,
a snowstorm began,
first softly, a few starry flakes,
then swiftly, as the wind rose,
and a thick curtain of white hid the outline of the river.

Father Pierre could see nothing
but the snow beneath his feet,
the snow ahead of him,
the snow about him,
but he toiled on and on,
winding here, turning there,
sometimes circling back on his own lost footsteps.

At night he dug a hole in the snow
under the shore of an island.
There, without fire or food or blanket,
he lay down.

At daybreak they sought him—
the captain of the fort,
the soldiers of the king of France,
a Huron Indian.
They tracked through the wilderness,
they fired guns, they shouted,
they beat down snow-laden pine trees.

On the second day they found him.
A distance above the fort, when weakness had dimmed
    his eyes,
he had knelt,
head bare,
and dug his resting place.
His hat and his snowshoes were at his side.
His hands, still clasping his rosary,
were clutched against his breast.

In Canada now
the name of Father Pierre
is unforgotten.
Children speak of him with reverence,
as they speak
of Anthony Daniel
and Gabriel Lalemant
and Jean de Brébeuf
and Isaac Jogues,
and all the other Jesuit martyrs
who became saints,
as they speak
of the holy men who came from
Ireland and England and Scotland
and other lands beyond the sea
to do the work of God
in Canada.

Along the shores of many rivers in many lands men have searched for gold. None sought it more eagerly than the mythical King Midas, whose greed for gold is the basis of the story

The Golden Touch

NATHANIEL HAWTHORNE

Once upon a time there lived a very rich man, and a king besides, whose name was Midas; and he had a little daughter, whom nobody but myself ever heard of, and whose name I either never knew, or have entirely forgotten. So, because I love odd names for little girls, I choose to call her Marygold.

This King Midas was fonder of gold than of anything else in the world. If he loved anything better, or half so well, it was the one little maiden who played so merrily around her father's footstool. But the more Midas loved his daughter, the more did he desire and seek for wealth.

He thought, foolish man! that the best thing he could possibly do for this dear child would be to give to her the biggest pile of yellow, glistening coin that had ever been heaped together since the world was made. Thus, he gave all his thoughts to this one purpose.

Now it happened that he chanced to befriend a stranger; and when he was asked to choose some good gift in return, he prayed that everything he touched might be turned to gold. The stranger smiled a little when he heard this foolish prayer.

"The Golden Touch!" he exclaimed. "Are you quite sure that this will satisfy you?"

"How could it fail?" asked Midas.

"And you will never regret the possession of it?"

"What would make me?" asked Midas. "I ask nothing else to make me perfectly happy."

"Be that as you wish, then," replied the stranger, waving his hand in farewell. "Tomorrow, at sunrise, you will find yourself gifted with the Golden Touch."

Day had hardly peeped over the hills, when Midas was broad awake and, stretching his arms out of bed, began to touch the objects that were within reach.

He seized one of the bedposts, and it immediately became a golden pillar. He pulled aside a window curtain, and the tassel became a mass of gold. He hurriedly put on his clothes, and was enraptured to see himself in a magnificent suit of gold cloth. He drew out his handkerchief which Marygold had hemmed for him. That was likewise gold, with the dear child's neat and pretty stitches running all along the border, in gold thread.

Somehow or other, this last change did not quite please King Midas. He would rather that his little daughter's gift should have remained just the same as when she climbed his knee and put it into his hand.

But it was not worth while to worry himself about a trifle. The king was so happy about his good fortune that the palace seemed too small to contain him. Therefore he went downstairs and out into the garden. Here he found a great number of beautiful roses.

But Midas knew a way to make them far more precious, according to his way of thinking, than roses had ever been before. He went from bush to bush, touching the blossoms, until every one was turned to gold.

By the time this work was done, King Midas was called to breakfast and he made haste back to the palace.

The breakfast consisted of hot cakes, some nice little brook trout, roasted potatoes, fresh boiled eggs, and coffee for King Midas himself. There was a bowl of bread and milk for his daughter, Marygold.

Little Marygold had not yet appeared; so her father ordered her to be called. Then he awaited the child's coming, in order to begin his own breakfast.

It was not a great while before he heard her coming. She was crying bitterly. This surprised him, because Marygold was always cheerful and almost never cried.

"How now, my little lady!" said Midas. "Pray what is the matter this bright morning?"

Marygold held out her hand. She had one of the roses which Midas had so recently turned into gold.

"Beautiful!" exclaimed her father. "And why does this make you cry?"

"Ah, dear father!" sobbed the child, "it is not beautiful, but the ugliest flower that ever grew! As soon as I was dressed I ran into the garden to pick some roses for you, but, oh dear, dear me! What do you think has happened? All the beautiful roses, that smelled so sweet, are spoiled!"

"There, there, my dear little girl,—please don't cry about it!" said Midas. "Sit down and eat your bread and milk!" Midas was ashamed to tell his little daughter that he himself had caused her to feel so bad.

Midas poured out a cup of coffee, and the coffee-pot was gold when he set it down. He lifted a spoonful of coffee to his lips. The instant his lips touched the liquid, it became melted gold, and the next moment hardened into a lump!

"Ha!" exclaimed Midas, rather frightened.

"What is the matter, father?" asked little Marygold. The tears were still standing in her eyes.

"Nothing, child, nothing!" said Midas. "Eat your bread and milk, like a good little girl."

He took one of the nice little trout on his plate and touched its tail with his finger. To his horror, it was immediately changed into a fish of gold. Its little bones were now golden wires and its fins and tail were thin pieces of gold.

He took one of the smoking-hot cakes. He had scarcely broken it when it changed to gold. Almost in despair, he helped himself to a boiled egg. The egg immediately changed as had the trout and cake.

He next snatched a hot potato. He tried to cram it into his mouth and swallow it in a hurry. But the Golden Touch was too quick for him. He found his mouth full, not of potato, but of solid metal. This so burnt his tongue that he cried aloud and jumped up from the table. He began to dance and stamp about the room, with both pain and fright.

"Father, dear father!" cried little Marygold, "what is the matter? Have you burnt your mouth?"

"Ah, dear child," groaned Midas, "I don't know what is to become of your poor father!"

And what was to be done? Already, at breakfast, Midas was hungry. Would he be less so at dinnertime? And what of supper? And the days to follow?

These thoughts so troubled King Midas that he began to doubt whether, after all, riches are the one desirable thing in the world. So great was his hunger and the seriousness of his state that he groaned aloud.

Pretty little Marygold could stand it no longer. She ran to her father and threw her arms about his knees. He bent down and kissed her. He felt that his little daughter's love was worth a thousand times more than he had gained by the Golden Touch.

"My precious, precious Marygold!" cried he.

But Marygold made no answer.

Alas, what had he done? How fatal was the gift which the stranger had given! The moment the lips of Midas touched Marygold's forehead, a change had taken place. Her sweet, rosy face, so full of affection as it had been, became a glittering yellow color, with yellow teardrops hardening on her cheeks. Her beautiful brown curls took the same tint. Her soft and tender little form grew hard and stiff within her father's encircling arms. Oh, terrible misfortune! The victim of his own greed for wealth, little Marygold was a human child no longer, but a golden statue!

Yes, there she was, with the questioning look of

love, grief, and pity, hardened into her face. It was the prettiest and most woeful sight that ever mortal saw. All the features of Marygold were there; even the beloved little dimple remained in her golden chin. But, the more perfect was the resemblance, the greater was the father's agony at beholding this golden image, which was all that was left him of a daughter. It had been a favorite phrase of Midas, whenever he felt particularly fond of the child, to say that she was worth her weight in gold. And now the phrase had become literally true.

King Midas could only wring his hands in despair. He wished he was the poorest man in the wide world, if the loss of all his wealth might bring back the faintest rose-color to his dear child's face.

While he was in the depths of despair, he suddenly beheld the stranger standing near the door. Midas bent down his head, without speaking, as he recognized the man who had appeared to him the day before and had given him the gift of the Golden Touch.

"Well, friend Midas," said the stranger, "pray how do you succeed with the Golden Touch?"

Midas shook his head. "I am very miserable," said he.

"Very miserable, indeed!" exclaimed the stranger. "And how does that happen? Have I not faithfully kept my promise to you? Have you not everything that your heart desires?"

"Gold is not everything," answered Midas. "I have lost all that my heart really cared for."

"You are wiser than you were, King Midas!" said the stranger, looking seriously at him. "Tell me, now, do you sincerely wish to rid yourself of this Golden Touch?"

"It is hateful to me!" replied Midas.

"Which of these two things do you think is really worth the more," asked the stranger, "the gift of the Golden Touch, or one cup of clear, cold water?"

"O blessed water!" exclaimed Midas.

"The Golden Touch," continued the stranger, "or a crust of bread?"

"A piece of bread," answered Midas, "is worth all the gold on earth!"

"The Golden Touch," asked the stranger, "or your own little Marygold, warm, soft, and loving as she was an hour ago?"

"Oh, my child, my dear child!" cried poor Midas, wringing his hands. "I would not have given that one small dimple in her chin for the power of changing this whole big earth into a lump of gold!"

"Your heart, I see, has not changed to gold," said the stranger. "So go and plunge into the river that glides at the edge of your garden. Take a vase of the same river water and sprinkle it over any object that you may desire to change back again from gold into its former substance."

King Midas bowed low; and when he lifted his head, the stranger had vanished. Midas lost no time in snatching up a large vase and hastening to the river.

On reaching the bank, he plunged headlong and washed away the Golden Touch.

Then he filled his vase and hastened back to the palace. The first thing he did, as you need hardly be told, was to sprinkle the water by handfuls over the golden figure of the little Marygold.

No sooner did it fall on her than you could have laughed to see how the rosy color came back to the dear child's cheek! and how she began to sneeze and sputter! —and how astonished she was to find herself dripping wet, and her father still throwing more water over her!

"Pray do not, dear father!" she cried. "See how you have wet my nice dress, which I put on only this morning!"

For Marygold did not know that she had been a little golden statue; nor could she remember anything that had happened since the moment when she ran with outstretched arms to comfort poor King Midas.

Her father did not tell his beloved child how very foolish he had been, but contented himself with showing how much wiser he had now grown. So he led little Marygold into the garden, where he sprinkled all the rest of the water over the rosebushes, and with such good effect that about five thousand roses recovered their beautiful bloom.

All that was left for the rest of his life to remind King Midas of his terrible greed were the sands of the river and the bright gleam in Marygold's hair.

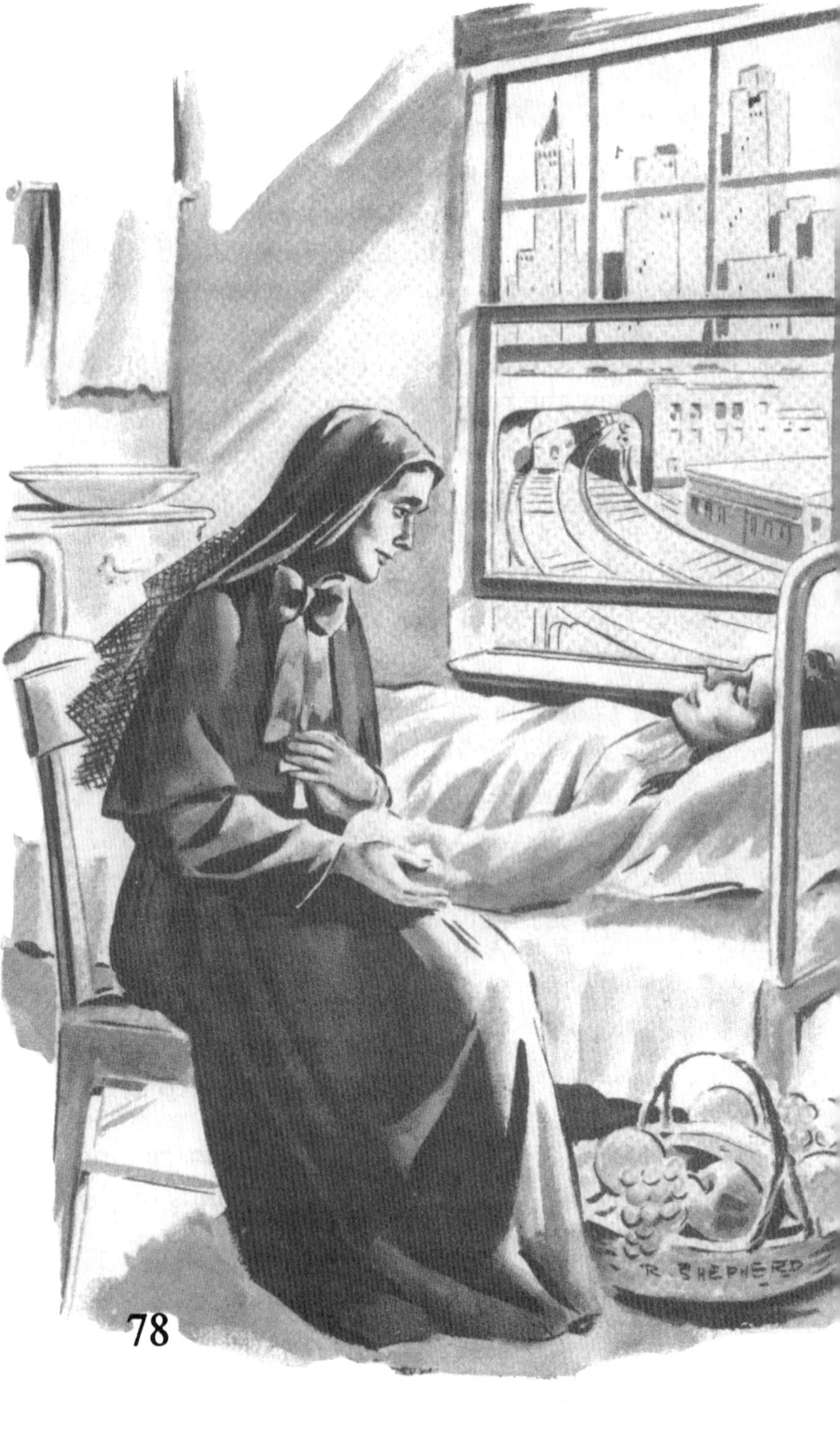
R. SHEPHERD

Saints of the Wide Roads

There are many saints of town and turnpike.

There is Saint Roch, who cared for the poor
and fed little children
and comforted the sick
as he walked and walked
the long, weary road to Rome.
With him, all the way, close at his heels,
trotted his little dog.

There is Saint Catherine of Siena,
who lived in the gentle beauty
of an old Italian city.
She knew and loved the needy.
She gave her silver cross to a beggar.
She gave her cloak to a shivering woman.
Saint Catherine loved the poor
because she loved Jesus Christ.

Around the throne of God
are countless holy men
and holy women
who were brave and good and kind.
Some of these saints have been in heaven
a long, long time.
One of them came but yesterday.
She is Mother Cabrini,
Saint Frances Xavier Cabrini.

She was such a quiet, simple woman.
She walked the city streets
of her adopted land,
dark streets, poor streets,
New York streets,
Chicago streets,
Seattle streets,
through sleet and snow and rain.
She helped tired women,
who were weary of their burden.
She fed the poor.
She led troubled souls
through mists of doubt and fear
back to God.
She begged for help that others might live.
She worked in city hospitals
long before gray dawns
rose over city roof tops.
She worked among the sick and dying
while cities slept.

Now, with all the saints in heaven,
Saint Frances Xavier Cabrini
looks down with compassion
upon the weary,
upon the poor,
upon the sinful
of town and turnpike,
for, always, she will be their friend.

White Fields

JAMES STEPHENS

[Choir to be arranged in three voices: high, medium, and low.]

All

    In the winter time we go
Walking in the fields of snow;

High

    Where there is no grass at all;
Where the top of every wall,

Medium, high   Every fence, and every tree,
Is as white as white could be.

Low

    Pointing out the way we came,

High

    —Every one of them the same—

Low

    All across the fields there be
Prints in silver filigree;

Medium, high   And our mothers always know,
By the footprints in the snow,

All

    Where it is the children go.

Just one hundred years ago this story of the rock-crystal mountain was written and published by a Bohemian writer as "a Christmas offering." Though it has been republished since then under other titles, he called it

Holy Eve

ADALBERT STIFTER

Among the high mountains of Austria there lies a little village called Rosenbush, right in the center of a broad valley.

No roads lead through the valley, so the villagers form a world by themselves. They all know one another by name and their family histories down from the time of grandfather and great-grandfather. They all mourn when one of them dies. They know what name the newborn babe will receive. They even have a language unlike that of the plains beyond.

To the south of the village there is a snow-mountain which lifts its rock-crystal peaks high above the roofs of the houses. The rise of the mountain is made from the valley. There is a high mountain ridge covered with pines which the villagers call "the neck." Over this neck one passes from one valley to another beyond the mountains. At its highest peak, where the path begins to drop to the valley below, there stands a post erected to mark the scene of a snow tragedy and to warn the traveler. Once upon a time a baker was found dead there. His picture is painted on the sign with a request for prayers for his soul. At this post, then, the careful traveler leaves the path and goes along the ridge of "the neck" instead of crossing it.

On the other side of the neck, in the valley beyond, is the busy town of Millsdorf.

Now, the natives of the little village of Rosenbush rarely leave their valley, even to travel across the mountain to Millsdorf. So, when the dyer's daughter from Millsdorf became the wife of the shoemaker of Rosenbush, she was considered a stranger to his fellow-townsmen. They never did her any harm; they even loved her for her beautiful ways, yet they always kept their distance, even after her son and daughter were born in Rosenbush.

At first, the grandmother from Millsdorf would cross the mountain to see Conrad the boy, and Susanna the girl. But when her age and health no longer permitted her to take such a long journey, the children were old enough to visit her.

Thus it happened that the two children made the way over the pass more often than all the other villagers; and because their mother had always been treated as a stranger in Rosenbush, the children had grown up to be strangers' children to the village folk. They felt they belonged to Millsdorf.

One winter, on the morning before Christmas, the shoemaker's wife said to her children, "As today is fine and pleasant, you may go to visit your grandmother in Millsdorf." When they were warmly dressed and ready, she added, "Now, Conrad, be careful of yourself and your little sister. Leave grandmother's early and come home; for the days are very short now and the sun sets very soon."

Conrad and Susanna said farewell to their mother and father. Then they rushed down the village street, passed over the square and along the rows of houses, and finally sped past the railings of the orchards out into the open.

There was no snow in the entire valley, but the higher mountains had been a-glisten with it for many weeks and were now all covered with a blanket of white.

The children reached the edge of the woods and walked on through them.

When they had climbed up into the higher woodlands of "the neck," the long furrows of the path were firm and frozen over with ice. When, after an hour's time, they had come to the top of "the neck," the ground was so hard that their steps clattered on the ice.

They came to the post that marked the scene of the death of the baker. It was Susanna who noticed that the post had fallen, but they said a prayer for the baker and moved on.

After another hour they had passed through the forest and were running through the meadows of the valley of Millsdorf.

Grandmother had seen them coming and had gone to meet them. She warmed them at the fire, she fed them, she talked with them and laughed with them, and then she said, "The day is short and it is growing colder. You must hurry back home."

When they were ready to leave she packed Conrad's knapsack with wheat bread to eat on the way, and with hot black coffee in a bottle for his mother. Also in Susanna's little pocket she put many small Christmas gifts. Then again she bade them go. "Greet father and mother and wish them a merry Christmas," she said.

The children walked past the cakes of ice beside grandfather's mill, passed through the fields of Millsdorf, and turned upward toward the meadows.

As they reached the heights, it began to snow.

Conrad and Susanna were very happy. They stepped on the soft white carpet and caught the light flakes in their outstretched hands.

A great stillness had set in. There was nothing to be seen of any bird. The whole forest seemed deserted.

"Shall we find the post?" asked Susanna. "You know that it had fallen down."

"We shall be able to see it," Conrad told her. "It is such a big thick post."

They walked on and on, but they could not see the post.

Conrad pulled up his jacket around his throat and pulled down his hat. He also fastened Susanna's scarf around her head so that the thickly falling snow would not wet her hair.

Still they had not reached the post.

"Shall we come to it soon?" asked the girl.

"I do not know," said the boy, but his voice was brave.

After a long time they still had not reached the height where the post was supposed to be, and from where the road was to go down into the village of Rosenbush.

"I see no more trees," said Susanna.

"We shall be all right," said Conrad, as he took his little sister by the hand and marched on.

The girl with her trusting blue eyes looked out on the whirling snow and gladly followed him.

Thus they went on, but as they trudged through the drifts they did not know whether they were going up the mountain or down.

"Where are we, Conrad?" asked the girl.

"I do not know," he answered. "Let us stand for a moment and listen. Perhaps we might hear a sound from the valley, a dog, or a bell, or the mill, or a shout, something that we must hear, and then we shall know which way to go."

They stood, but they heard nothing.

Then they went on again.

After a time they saw rocks that rose up like walls, walls so steep that not a flake of snow could cling to them.

"Where are we?" cried Susanna.

"I do not know," sighed Conrad, "but do not be afraid. I shall lead you safely home."

They came to huge formations of ice that looked like the frozen bed of some great torrent. Before them yawned a cavern bluer than the sky, thick with frosty icicles. It would have been pleasant to stay in the blue cave, for no snow could come in, but it was so fearfully blue that the children took fright and ran out again.

They passed along the ice, thrusting their little bodies into every crevice, creeping where they could not walk, climbing ever higher in the hope of reaching some height where they could look down and see the village.

But only slabs and spires of ice rose about them.

"Susanna, we cannot make our way here," said the boy.

"No," she said, and there was fear in her young voice.

"Then we will turn back and try to go down somewhere else."

"Yes, Conrad."

They turned hither and thither, but everywhere there was ice.

And it was growing dark.

At the tip of the glacier there were some scattered rocks piled in huge heaps, and over them lay broad slabs like a roof.

"We shall go in under those stones where it is dry," said Conrad, "and we shall wait there until morning. The sun will rise, and then we shall run down the mountain. Don't cry, please don't cry, and I shall give you all the things to eat which grandmother gave us."

The little girl did not cry. She sat down beneath the rocky roof and she kept very quiet.

Conrad opened his knapsack, and both of them began to eat.

From that time on, as night fell and all was dark about them, the children sat and looked at the high, bright stars, and said their prayers.

This was the moment when people in the valleys lighted their Christmas candles. At this hour, the children in all the valleys were receiving their Christmas presents, but these two little ones sat alone up there by the edge of the glacier, with no light but the light of the stars.

After a long time the boy said, "Susanna, you must not sleep, for father says that if one sleeps in the mountains, one will freeze to death."

"I shall not sleep," said the little girl feebly.

Conrad reached for his knapsack, opened it, groped around it until he found the little bottle in which grandmother had put black coffee for mother. "Taste this," he said. "It will keep you warm."

Susanna took a swallow of the coffee. Then the boy drank a little, too.

So the long night passed and, at last, day came.

The children arose. The sun was shining in all its beauty on the snowy heights yet, even in bright daylight, all places looked alike. Snow and snow again, but the children trudged on and on.

At last, when all hope seemed gone, the boy thought he saw a flame skipping over a far-away snow slope. It bobbed up and dipped down again. Then, after a while, they heard in the still air the long note of a shepherd's horn. As if from instinct, the children shouted aloud. They shouted again and remained standing on the same spot. The flame came nearer. The sound of the horn was heard again, and this time more plainly. The children answered, shouting. After a time, they knew it was no flame they had seen, but a red flag that was being swung. Then came once more the call of the shepherd's horn.

"Susanna," cried the boy, "there come people from Rosenbush."

For the children could see people near the flag.

Over the snow slope came the villagers—the shepherd Philip with his horn, his two sons, a young hunter, and many men of Rosenbush. "God be blessed," cried Philip, "you are safe. The whole mountain is full of people. Let someone run down and ring the great mountain bell that all will know the children have been found."

"Let someone climb the peak and plant the flag so that watchers in the valley may see it and fire off the guns, so that the men searching in the Millsdorf forest may hear them," cried the hunter.

"Let them light the smudge fires in Rosenbush!" cried the shepherd's son. "This is a Christmas for you!"

One of Philip's sons led the way downward, and the hunter took Susanna by the hand, and the shepherd helped the weary boy. Thus they started out. Now they climbed up, now they climbed down, through snow, over steep inclines, and they heard the great mountain bell ring, and they heard the thunder of gunfire, and finally they saw thin columns of smoke from the smudge pots of Rosenbush.

Halfway up the last small hill the mother of the children was waiting for them. "Sebastian, here they are!" she sobbed, as she rushed to welcome them.

Behind her came the shoemaker. Catching his children in his arms and holding them, he tried to voice his gratitude to the men who had saved them. "Neighbors and friends, I thank you!" was all that he could say because of tears.

Neighbors and friends!

No longer was the daughter of the dyer of Millsdorf a stranger in Rosenbush.

From that day on Conrad and Susanna, too, really felt that they belonged in the village where they had been born, for men had risked their lives to save them and had lifted flags of gladness and lighted fires of victory for them.

As they crossed the meadows of Rosenbush on that bright Christmas morning they heard the bell in the village church ringing in the happy day.

"Praise be the Lord," said the children's mother, as she made the Sign of the Cross.

"May His name be ever blessed," said the shoemaker, and bowed his head in grateful prayer.

There is an old legend which asserts that dumb animals not only kneel in their stalls on Christmas Eve, but also speak among themselves.
The little brown nut, Miss Hickory, talks with the animals as they travel toward the Light in the woods, in the story

Now Christmas Comes

CAROLYN SHERWIN BAILEY

Now, the day before Christmas, Miss Hickory felt that something was in the air. Not a feeling that could be put into words, or even worked out in her mind. Nothing was changed, but the fields and the forest seemed expectant. Snow lay deep, but it was crisscrossed and mapped by the marks of small hurrying feet, rabbits, winter birds, and deer.

Miss Hickory remembered last Christmas. She had lived then on the kitchen window sill of the Old Place. There, she had sniffed mince pies, turkey, and Christmas pudding, the Christmas tree in the parlor, and boiling molasses taffy. But her life was so changed now that last Christmas was only the dimmest memory.

That was why Miss Hickory did not believe Squirrel. He dashed up-boughs to her nest as it began to be dusk. "Full moon tonight, Miss Hickory," he announced. "Bright moonlight for Christmas Eve. You mustn't go to bed too early. Stay up for the celebration."

"What celebration?" Miss Hickory pulled her hat down tightly. Even now, after so many weeks, she did not really trust Squirrel.

Stopping by Woods on a Snowy Evening

ROBERT FROST

Whose woods these are I think I know.
His house is in the village though;
He will not see me stopping here
To watch his woods fill up with snow.

My little horse must think it queer
To stop without a farmhouse near
Between the woods and frozen lake
The darkest evening of the year.

He gives his harness bells a shake
To ask if there is some mistake.
The only other sound's the sweep
Of easy wind and downy flake.

The woods are lovely, dark and deep.
But I have promises to keep,
And miles to go before I sleep,
And miles to go before I sleep.

Song of the Brook

ALFRED, LORD TENNYSON

I come from haunts of coot and hern,
    I make a sudden sally,
And sparkle out among the fern,
    To bicker down a valley.

By thirty hills I hurry down,
    Or slip between the ridges,
By twenty thorps, a little town,
    And half a hundred bridges.

I chatter over stony ways,
    In little sharps and trebles,
I bubble into eddying bays,
    I babble on the pebbles.

With many a curve my banks I fret
    By many a field and fallow,
And many a fairy foreland set
    With willow-weed and mallow.

I chatter, chatter, as I flow
    To join the brimming river,
For men may come and men may go,
    But I go on forever.

I wind about, and in and out,
    With here a blossom sailing,
And here and there a lusty trout,
    And here and there a grayling,

And here and there a foamy flake
  Upon me, as I travel
With many a silvery water-break
  Above the golden gravel,

And draw them all along, and flow
  To join the brimming river,
For men may come and men may go,
  But I go on forever.

I steal by lawns and grassy plots,
  I slide by hazel covers;
I move the sweet forget-me-nots
  That grow for happy lovers.

I slip, I slide, I gloom, I glance
  Among my skimming swallows;
I make the netted sunbeam dance
  Against my sandy shallows.

I murmur under moon and stars
  In brambly wildernesses;
I linger by my shingly bars;
  I loiter round my cresses;

And out again I curve and flow
  To join the brimming river,
For men may come and men may go,
  But I go on forever.

Ships

NANCY BYRD TURNER

[Choir to be arranged in three voices: high, medium, and low.]

Medium   Go out, good ships, across the tide,
Low   Be brave to meet all weathers;
Medium, high Make many a port, and fill each hold
            With sky-blue silk and yellow gold
All   And pearls and peacock feathers.

Medium   The wind is in your shining sails,
Low   Your keen prows cut the foam;
High   Sail very fast and very far,
            Then turn,
All   and by the Northern Star
            Come steering safely home.

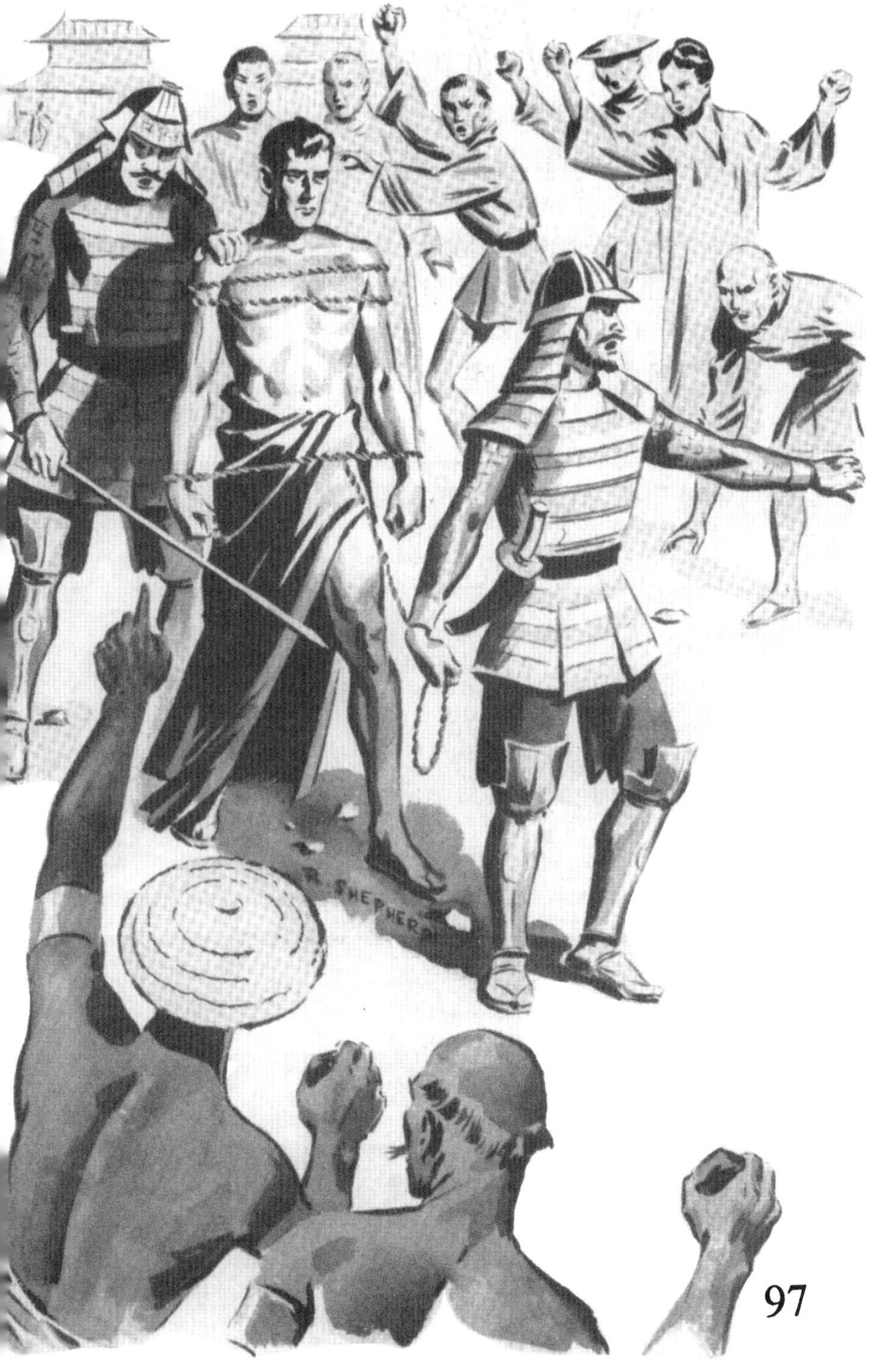
R. SHEPHERD

First Saint of the Americas

At high Mass on the feast day
of Saint Philip of Jesus,
red robes of martyrdom are worn;
red for Christian blood
shed in the cities of Japan,
in Kyoto, in Osaka;
red for the blood on the spear
thrust into the side
of the first American saint
who died on the Mount of Martyrs
above Nagasaki,
more than three hundred years ago.

Saint Philip of Jesus—
Mexico calls him San Felipe de las Casas—
never saw an airplane.
He would have laughed
at the thought
of flight by air.
In Mexico City, where he was born,
there were ways of transportation—
there were little donkeys
harnessed to little carts;
there were blooded horses,
decked with saddles whose trim
was gold and silver;
there were carriages
of Spanish noblemen;

there were galleons,
the ships of the Spanish fleet.

A boy who earned
but five cents a day
in the shop of a silversmith,
had little time, and no money,
for donkeys or carts or blooded horses.
Work was hard. Hours were long.
So Philip ran away.
He came to the sea, to a harbor
on the west coast of Mexico;
there, its sails set,
he saw the Spanish galleon.
The gay songs of the sailors,
the friendliness of the captain,
the wide track of the western sea,
stirred the heart
of the lonely boy;
with the ebbing of the tide
he sailed with them toward the East.

In a year, older, wiser,
tired of storms,
tired of strife,
and eager to serve God,
Philip sought the Franciscans
in a monastery in Manila.
He studied. He worked. He prayed.

Then, ready for his ordination,
he sailed for the great cathedral
in Mexico, the land of his birth.
With him went another Franciscan,
two Augustinians, and a Dominican.

On the Feast of the Immaculate Conception
a storm drove their ship
upon the coast of Japan.
The Emperor, enraged,
thinking it was invasion,
seized them, arrested them,
sentenced them to death.
They were paraded through the streets of Kyoto.
They were jeered in Osaka.
They were taken to the hill above Nagasaki.
There, bound upon crosses,
they were pierced with spears.
Now the priest in a red robe
prays on the feast day of Saint Philip
that he, and all the holy martyrs,
may be our advocates in heaven.

The Ships of Yule

BLISS CARMAN

When I was just a little boy,
Before I went to school,
I had a fleet of forty sail
I called the Ships of Yule;

Of every rig, from rakish brig
And gallant barkentine,
To little Fundy fishing boats
With gunwales painted green.

They used to go on trading trips
Around the world for me,
For though I had to stay on shore
My heart was on the sea.

They stopped at every port of call
From Babylon to Rome,
To load with all the lovely things
We never had at home;

With elephants and ivory
Bought from the King of Tyre,
And shells and silk and sandalwood
That sailormen admire;

With figs and dates from Samarcand
And squatty ginger-jars,
And scented silver amulets
From Indian bazaars;

With sugar cane from Port of Spain,
And monkeys from Ceylon,
And paper lanterns from Pekin
With painted dragons on;

With coconuts from Zanzibar,
And pines from Singapore;
And when they had unloaded these
They could go back for more.

And even after I was big
And had to go to school,
My mind was often far away
Aboard the Ships of Yule.

An old gypsy legend says that the gypsies gave shelter
to Mary and Joseph and the Christ Child
as the Holy Family fled into Egypt from the wrath of Herod.
This is their story of

The First Birthday

RUTH SAWYER

It was winter—and twelve months since the gypsies had driven their flocks of mountain sheep over the dark, gloomy Balkan mountains, and had settled in the southland. It was twelve months since they had seen a wonderful star appear in the sky and heard the singing of angelic voices afar off.

They had wondered much about the star until a runner had passed them from the south bringing them news that the star had marked the birth of a Child whom the wise men had hailed as "King of Israel" and "Prince of

Peace." This had made Herod, the King of Judea, both afraid and angry, and he had sent soldiers secretly to kill the Child; but in the night they had miraculously disappeared—the Child with Mary and Joseph—and no one knew whither they had gone. Therefore Herod had sent runners all over the lands that bordered the sea with a message forbidding everyone to give food or shelter or warmth to the Child, under penalty of death. For Herod's anger was far-reaching, and where his anger fell, there fell his sword likewise. Having given his warning, the runner passed on, leaving the gypsies to marvel much over the tale they had heard and the meaning of the star.

Now, on that day that marked the end of the twelve months since the star had shone, the gypsies said among themselves, "Dost thou think that the star will shine again tonight? If it were true, what the runner said, that when it shone twelve months ago it marked the place where the Child was born it may even mark His hiding-place this night. Then Herod would know where to find Him and send his soldiers again to slay Him. That would be a cruel thing to happen!"

The air was chill with the winter frost, even there in the southland; and the gypsies built high their fire and hung their kettle full of fish and bitter herbs for their supper. The king lay on his couch of tigerskins and on his arms were charms of heavy gold, while rings of gold were on his fingers and in his ears. His robe was of heavy silk covered with a leopard cloak, and on his feet were shoes of goatskin trimmed with fur. Now as they feasted around the fire, a voice came to them through the darkness, calling. It was a man's voice, climbing the mountains from the south.

"Ohe! Ohe!" he shouted. And then nearer, "O—he!"

The gypsies were still arguing among themselves whence the voice came when there walked into the circle about the fire a tall, kindly man and a sweet-faced young mother, carrying a child.

"We are outcasts," said the man hoarsely. "Ye must know that whosoever helps us will bring Herod's anger like a sword about his head. For a year we have wandered homeless over the world. Only the wild creatures have not feared to share their food and give us shelter in their dens. But tonight we can go no farther; and we beg the warmth of your fire and food enough to stay us until the morrow."

The king looked at them long before he made reply. He saw the weariness in their eyes and the hunger in their cheeks; he saw, as well, the holy light that hung about the child, and he said at last to his men, "It is the Child of Bethlehem, the one they call the 'Prince of Peace.' As the man says, who shelters them shelters the anger of Herod as well. Shall we let them stay?"

One of their number sprang to his feet, crying, "It is a sin to turn strangers from the fire, a greater sin if they be poor and friendless. And what is a king's anger to us? I say bid them welcome. What say the rest?"

And with one voice the gypsies shouted, "Yea, let them stay!"

They brought fresh skins and threw them down beside the fire for the man and woman to rest on. They brought them food and wine, and goat's milk for the Child; and when they had seen that all was made comfortable for them they gathered round the Child—these dark gypsy men—to touch His small, white hands and feel His golden hair. They brought Him a chain of gold to play with and another for His neck and tiny arm.

"See, these shall be Thy gifts, little one," said they, "the gifts for Thy first birthday."

And long after all had fallen asleep the Child lay on His bed of skins beside the blazing fire and watched the light dance on the beads of gold. He laughed and clapped His hands together to see the pretty sight they made; and then a bird called out of the woods close by.

"Little Child of Bethlehem," it called, "I, too, have a birth gift for Thee. I will sing Thy cradle song this night." And softly, like the tinkling of a silver bell and like clear water running over mossy places, the nightingale sang and sang, filling the air with melodies.

And then another voice called to him, "Little Child of Bethlehem, I am only a tree with boughs all bare, for the winter has stolen my green cloak, but I also can give Thee a birth gift. I can give Thee shelter from the biting north wind that blows." And the tree bent low its branches and twined a rooftree and a wall about the Child.

Soon the Child was fast asleep, and while He slept a small brown bird hopped out of the wood. Cocking his little head, he said, "What can I be giving the Child of Bethlehem? I could fetch Him a fat worm to eat or catch Him the beetle that crawls on yonder bush, but He would not like that! And I could tell Him a story of the lands of the north, but He is asleep and would not hear." And the brown bird shook its head quite sorrowfully. Then it saw that the wind was bringing the sparks from the fire nearer and nearer to the sleeping Child.

"I know what I can do," said the bird joyously. "I can catch the hot sparks on my breast, for if one should fall upon the Child it would burn Him."

So the small, brown bird spread wide his wings and caught the sparks on his own brown breast. So many fell that the feathers were burned; and burned was the flesh beneath until the breast was no longer brown, but red.

The next morning, when the gypsies awoke, they found Mary and Joseph and the Child gone. For Herod had died, and an angel had come in the night and told Joseph to go back to the land of Judea. But the good God blessed those who had cared that night for the Child.

To the nightingale He said, "Your song shall be the sweetest in all the world, for ever and ever; and only you shall sing the long night through."

To the tree He said, "Little fir tree, never more shall your branches be bare. Winter and summer you and your seedlings shall stay green, ever green."

Last of all He blessed the brown bird: "Faithful little watcher, from this night forth you and your children shall have red breasts, that the world may never forget your gift to the Child of Bethlehem."

A Carol for Sleepy Children

SISTER MARIS STELLA

When Mary came to Bethlehem
   On the first Christmas night,
She bore the lovely Christ Child
   To be each child's delight.

There was no room in Bethlehem
   For anyone so small
And yet so great as Mary's Child
   But in an ox's stall.

There was no bed in Bethlehem
   For anyone so poor
And yet so rich as Mary's Child
   But on the stable floor.

O all you little children
   Who sleep in linen white,
Would you not share your cradles,
   If Jesus came tonight?

In Switzerland, high up in the mountains,
a little girl named Heidi once came to live in a mountain hut
with her grandfather. As playmate and friend she found young Peter,
the goatherd. Together they led the goats to

The Mountain Pasture

JOHANNA SPYRI

The pasture where Peter usually went with his goats for the day lay at the foot of the high cliff. The lower part of this was covered with bushes and fir trees, but it rose toward heaven quite bare and steep. On one side of the mountain there were deep valleys. Heidi's grandfather had warned Peter about them, urging him to care for Heidi lest she fall.

When Peter reached this spot on the heights, he stretched himself out on the ground in the sunny pasture to rest from the labor of climbing. Heidi sat down and looked around her. The valley lay far below in the full morning sunshine. In front of her Heidi saw a great, wide field of snow, stretching high up into the deep-blue sky; on the left stood a great mass of rock, on each side of which a higher tower of bare, jagged cliffs rose into the sky and looked very sternly down on Heidi. The child sat as still as a mouse; everywhere there was a great, deep stillness; only the wind passed very softly and gently over the tender bluebells and the radiant golden rock-roses, which were everywhere gaily nodding to and fro on their slender stems.

She drank in the golden sunlight, the fresh air, the delicate fragrance of the flowers, and desired nothing more than to remain there forever. A good while passed in this way, and Heidi had gazed so often and so long at the lofty mountaintops that it seemed as if they all had faces and were gazing down quite familiarly at her, like good friends.

Suddenly Peter jumped up and fairly leaped after the goats. Heidi ran after him; she felt that something must have happened, and she could not remain behind. Peter ran through the midst of the goats to the side of the mountain, where the rocks descended steep and bare far below, and where a careless goat, going near, might easily fall over and break all its bones. He had seen the venturesome goat named Greenfinch jumping along in that direction; he reached there just in time, for at that instant the little goat came to the very edge of the cliff.

Just as it was falling, Peter flung himself down on the ground and managed to seize one of its legs and hold it fast. Greenfinch bleated with anger and surprise, to be held so by his leg and prevented from continuing his merry course, and struggled obstinately onward. Peter screamed, "Heidi, help me!" for he couldn't get up and was almost pulling off Greenfinch's leg. Heidi was already there and instantly understood their sorry plight. She quickly pulled up from the ground some fragrant herbs and held them under Greenfinch's nose and said soothingly, "Come, come, Greenfinch, you must be sensible! See, you might fall off and break your bones, and that would give you frightful pain."

The goat quickly turned round and eagerly nibbled the herbs from Heidi's hand. Meanwhile Peter had been able to rise on his feet and had seized the cord which held the bell round Greenfinch's neck. Heidi seized it on the opposite side, and the two together led the runaway back to the peacefully feeding flock.

When Peter had the goat in safety once more, he raised his rod to beat him soundly as a punishment, and Greenfinch timidly drew back, for he saw what was going to happen. But Heidi cried, "No, Peter! no, you must not beat him! See how frightened he is!"

"He deserves it," snarled Peter and he was going to strike the goat.

But Heidi seized his arm and cried indignantly, "You shall not do it; it will hurt him! Let him alone!"

Peter looked in astonishment at the commanding Heidi, whose black eyes snapped at him. He hesitatingly dropped his rod.

"He can go if tomorrow you will give me some of the cheese in your lunch," said Peter, yielding; for he wanted some reward for his fright.

"You may have it all—the whole piece—tomorrow and every day; I do not want it," said Heidi, ready to agree; "and I will give you a good part of my bread too, as I did today. But then you must never, never beat Greenfinch, nor any of the goats."

"It's all the same to me," remarked Peter; and this was as good as a promise with him. Then he let the guilty goat go, and the happy Greenfinch leaped high in the air and then bounded back into the flock.

Thus the day had passed away unnoticed, and the sun was just ready to go down behind the mountains. Heidi sat down on the ground again and silently gazed at the bluebells and the rock-roses glowing in the evening light. All the grass seemed tinted with gold, and the cliffs above began to gleam and sparkle. Suddenly Heidi jumped up and exclaimed, "Peter! Peter! It's on fire! It's on fire! All the mountains are burning, and the big snow-field over there is on fire, and the sky! Oh, see! see! The high cliff is all burning! Oh, the beautiful fiery snow! Peter, get up! Look at the rocks! See the fir trees! Everything, everything is on fire!"

"It's always so," said Peter good-naturedly, peeling the bark from his rod; "but it is no fire."

"What is it, then?" asked Heidi, running back and forth in order to look on every side; for she could not see enough, it was so beautiful everywhere.

"What is it, Peter? what is it?" cried Heidi again.

"It comes so of itself," explained Peter. "It is the sunset."

"Oh, see! see!" cried Heidi in great excitement; "suddenly it grows rosy red! Look at the snow and the high, pointed rocks! What are their names, Peter?"

"Mountains don't have names," he replied.

"Oh, but see the snow all rosy red! And oh, on the rocks above there are ever and ever so many roses! Oh, now they are turning gray! Oh! Oh! Now it is all gone! It is all gone, Peter!" And Heidi sat down on the ground and looked as sad as if everything were really coming to an end.

"It will be just the same again tomorrow," explained Peter. "Get up! We must go home now."

Peter whistled and called the goats together, and they started on the homeward journey.

"Will it be like that every day—every day when we go to the pasture?" asked Heidi eagerly as she walked down the mountain by Peter's side.

"Usually," was the reply.

"But really tomorrow again?" she wanted to know.

"Yes; yes, tomorrow, certainly!" said Peter.

Then Heidi was happy once more.

In the Fields

ELIZABETH BARRETT BROWNING

The little cares that fretted me,
I lost them yesterday
Among the fields above the sea,
Among the winds at play;
Among the lowing of the herds,
The rustling of the trees;
Among the singing of the birds,
The humming of the bees.

The foolish fears of what might happen—
I cast them all away
Among the clover-scented grass,
Among the new-mown hay;
Among the husking of the corn,
Where the drowsy poppies nod,
Where ill thoughts die and good are born,
Out in the fields with God.

Easter

CHRISTINA ROSSETTI

[Choir to be arranged in three voices: high, medium, and low.]

All Spring bursts today,
For Christ is risen and all earth's at play.

Low Flash forth, thou sun.
The rain is over and gone, its work is done.

All Winter is past,
Sweet spring is come at last, is come at last.

Low Break forth this morn
In roses, thou but yesterday a thorn.

Medium Uplift thy head,
O pure white lily, through the winter dead.

High Sing, creatures, sing,
Angels and men and birds and everything!

Easter

JOYCE KILMER

The air is like a butterfly
   With frail blue wings.
The happy earth looks at the sky
   And sings.

Sheep and Lambs

KATHARINE TYNAN

All in the April evening,
April airs were abroad;
The sheep with their little lambs
Passed me by on the road.

The sheep with their little lambs
Passed me by on the road;
All in the April evening
I thought on the Lamb of God.

The lambs were weary and crying
With a weak and human cry.
I thought on the Lamb of God
Going meekly out to die.

Up in the blue, blue mountains
Dewy pastures are sweet;
Rest for the little bodies,
Rest for the little feet.

But for the Lamb of God,
Up on the hill-top green,
Only a cross of shame
Two stark crosses between.

All in the April evening,
April airs were abroad;
I saw the sheep with their lambs,
And thought on the Lamb of God.

One of the reasons why Athens in Greece was
the greatest of all ancient cities was because men helped one another.
One great sculptor, Phidias, was famous not only for his art,
but also for his kindness. His story is

How Phidias Helped the Image-Maker

BEATRICE HARRADEN

It was in the year 450 B.C., in the early summer, and Phidias, who had been working all the day, strolled quietly along the streets of Athens.

As he passed the market place, he chanced to look up and he saw a young girl of about thirteen years sitting near him. Her face was of the purest beauty, but she looked poor and in distress. She came forward and begged for help; and there was something in her manner, as well as in her face, which made Phidias pause and listen to her.

"My father lies ill," she cried, not knowing she was speaking to the greatest sculptor in Athens, "and he cannot do his work, and so we can get no food—nothing to make him well and strong again. If I could only do his work for him I should not mind; and then I should not beg. He does not know I came out to beg—he would never forgive me; but I could not bear to see him lying there without food."

"And who is your father?" asked Phidias kindly.

"He is a maker of images—little clay figures of gods and goddesses and heroes. Indeed, he is clever; and I am sure you would praise the last statue he finished before he was taken ill. His name is Aristaeus."

"Take me to your home," Phidias said to the girl. As they passed on together he asked her many questions about the image-maker. She was proud of her father, and Phidias smiled to himself at her loyalty.

"Is it not wonderful," she said, "to take the clay and work it into forms? Not everyone could do that—could you do it?"

Phidias laughed. "Perhaps not so well as your father," he answered kindly. "Still, I can do it."

A sudden thought struck Iris. "Perhaps you would help father?" she said eagerly. "Ah! but I ought not to have said that."

"Perhaps I can help him," replied Phidias good-naturedly. "Anyway, take me to him."

She led him through some side streets into the poorest parts of the city and stopped before a little window, where a few rough images and vases were exposed to view. She beckoned to him to follow her and, opening the door, crept gently into a room which served as their workshop and dwelling-place. Phidias saw a man stretched out on a couch at the farther end of the room, near a bench where many images of all sorts lay unfinished.

"This is our home," whispered Iris proudly, "and that is my father yonder."

The image-maker looked up and called for Iris. "I am so faint, child," he murmured. "If I could only become strong again, I could get back to my work. It is so hard to lie here and die."

Phidias bent over him. "You shall not die," he said, "if money can do you any good. I met your little daughter, and she told me that you were an image-maker; and that interested me, because, I, too, can make images, though perhaps not so well as you. Still, I thought I should like to come and see you and help you. If you will let me, I will try to make a few images for you, so that your daughter may go out and sell them and bring you home money. And meanwhile, she shall fetch you some food to nourish you."

Then he turned to Iris and, putting some coins into her hands, told her to go out and bring what she thought fit. She did not know how to thank him, but hurried away on her glad errand, and Phidias talked kindly to his fellow-worker. Then, throwing aside his cloak, he sat down at the bench and began to model the clay.

It was so different from his usual work that he could not help smiling.

"This is easier," he thought to himself, "than carving from the marble a statue of Athena. What a strange occupation!" Nevertheless, he was so interested in modeling the quaint little images that he did not notice that Iris had returned until he looked up and saw her standing near him, watching him with wonder.

"Oh, how clever!" she cried. "Father, if you could only see what he is doing!"

"Nay, child," said the sculptor, laughing; "get your father his food and leave me to my work. I am going to model a little image of the goddess Athena, for I think the folk will like to buy that, since Phidias has set up his statue of her in the temple square."

"Phidias, the prince of sculptors!" said the sick image-maker. "May the gods preserve his life; for he is the greatest glory of all Athens."

"Yes," said Iris, as she prepared her father's food, "that is what we call him—the greatest glory of all Athens."

"We think of him," said the sick man, feebly, "and that helps us in our work. Yes, it helps even us poor image-makers. When I saw the beautiful Athena I came home cheered and encouraged. May Phidias be watched over and blessed all his life!"

The tears came into the eyes of Phidias as he bent over his work. It was a pleasure to him to think that his fame gained for him a resting-place of love and gratitude in the hearts of the poorest citizens of Athens. He valued this praise of the image-maker far more than that of the rich and great. Before he left he saw that both father and daughter were much refreshed by the food which he had given to them, and he told the elder man to be of good cheer because he would surely regain his health and strength.

"And because you love your art," he said, "I shall be a friend to you and help you. I shall come again tomorrow and do some work for you—that is to say, if you approve of what I have already done, and then Iris will be able to go out and sell the figures."

The next day Phidias came again and took his place at the image-maker's bench, just as if he were always accustomed to sit there. The elder man, who was better, watched him curiously, but asked no questions.

But Iris said to him, "My father and I talk of you and wonder who you are."

Phidias laughed. "Perhaps I shall tell you some day," he answered.

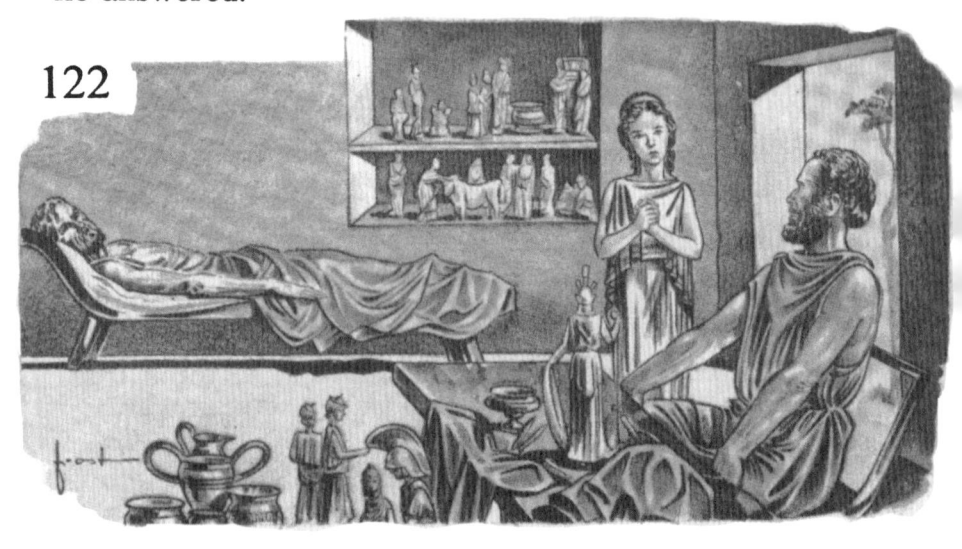

As the days went on, the image-maker recovered his strength; and meanwhile Phidias had filled the little shop with dainty images and graceful vases, such as had never been seen there before.

One evening, when her father and Iris were admiring the stranger's work, the door opened and Phidias came in.

"What, friend," he said cheerily, "you are better tonight, I see!"

"Last night," said the image-maker, "I dreamt that the friend who held out a brother's hand to me and helped me in my trouble was the great Phidias himself. It did not seem wonderful to me, for only the great do such things as you have done for me."

"I do not know about that," said the sculptor, smiling, "and after all, I have not done so much for you. I have only helped a brother-workman; for I am an image-maker too—and my name is Phidias."

Then Aristaeus bent down and reverently kissed the great sculptor's hands.

"I cannot find words with which to thank you," he murmured, "but the gods will forever bless Phidias."

And Phidias went on his way, many times richer and happier for the image-maker's words. For there is something lovelier than fame and wealth, my children; it is the opportunity of giving the best of one's self and the best of one's powers to help those of our fellow-workers who need our active help.

Beautiful Things

ANN TAYLOR

What millions of beautiful things there must be
In this mighty world!—who could reckon them all?
The tossing, the foaming, the wide flowing sea,
And thousands of rivers that into it fall.

O there are the mountains, half covered with snow,
With tall and dark trees, like a girdle of green,
And waters that wind in the valleys below,
Or roar in the caverns, too deep to be seen.

Here, spread the sweet meadows with thousands of flowers;
Far away are old woods, that for ages remain;
Wild elephants sleep in the shade of their bowers;
Or troops of young antelopes traverse the plain.

O yes, they are glorious, all, to behold,
And pleasant to read of, and curious to know,
And something of God and His wisdom we're told,
Whatever we look at—wherever we go!

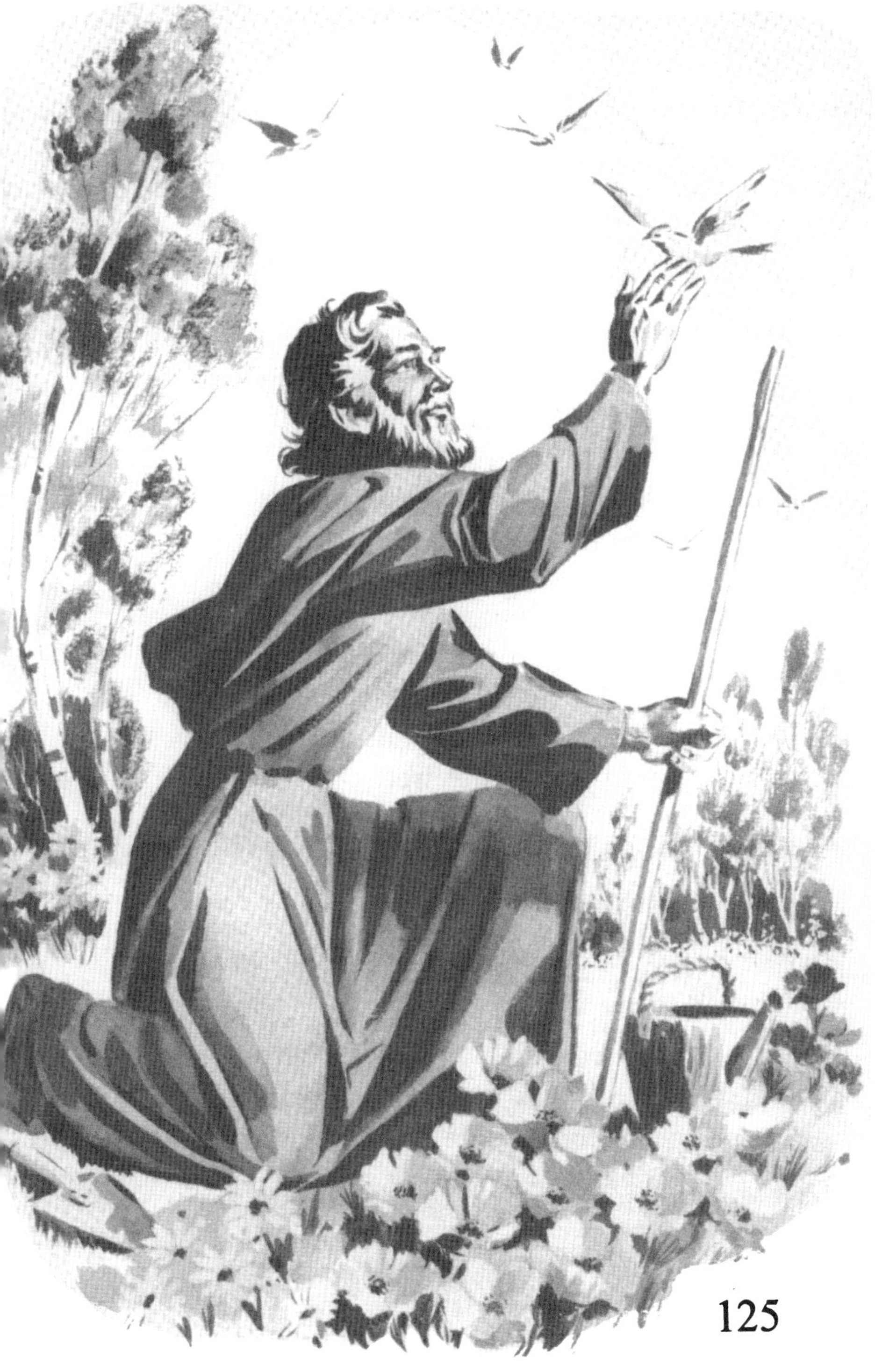

The Saint of Gardeners
A long time ago
in a wood
that was circled
by a ring of white birch trees,
there lived a hermit
whose name was Fiacre.
Fee-ak-er! Fee-ak-er! Fee-ak-er!
the birds called to him
as they soared and dipped
above the slim birch trees
in the bright spring morning.

Fiacre wore a brown robe,
an old, worn, brown robe,
as brown as the fur of a beaver,
as brown as the nuts
of the hazelnut tree,
and all that he did
the livelong day
was dig in a garden
beside a little brook,
and feed the poor,
who came to the garden gate.

The birds all knew that garden,
for long before winter snows
had melted into the brook,
the robin came.

Then, with flash of yellow
through silver birches,
came the oriole.
A blackbird whistled.
A blue jay screamed
and, with warble, with chirp,
with twitter and with trill,
all the birds of the wood cried,
Fee-ak-er! Fee-ak-er! Fee-ak-er!

In that garden,
beside a little brook,
the flowers were the loveliest
in all the land.
There were the bluest violets,
the whitest daisies,
the reddest poppies,
and the buttercups
were as golden as the sun.

All day long Fiacre dug
and planted
and weeded
and trimmed,
and the flowers grew brighter
and the beans grew stronger
and the pumpkins grew rounder
and the cabbage grew greener
and the carrots grew longer

and the cherries grew riper
and the pears grew sweeter
and the poor came from miles and miles
with their baskets over their arms
and they went away
with their baskets filled.

Fiacre lived such a quiet life
in the wood of the silver birches;
by night he prayed
as the red embers of his fire
turned to black,
and the birds slept;
by dawn he arose
and passed through
lily-green shadows
on to the sunlight,
where the vegetables ripened,
where the flowers bloomed,
and there he worked
until another day was done.

In the long and mighty roll
of the names of the saints,
you can find the name,
    Fiacre!
There it is, set down among saints
who once were popes
and kings.

All through the eastern provinces of Canada you see cities made great and land made fertile by the skill and labor of French-Canadian settlers. In the beautiful land of the Gaspé Peninsula, in the province of Quebec, there lives a little girl with her brother and her sisters and her uncle and her aunt. Her name is

Petite Suzanne

MARGUERITE DE ANGELI

Suzanne was anxious to start for school.

The school is just beyond the *bureau de poste*, where the mail comes. It is quite a long walk, down the road, through the covered bridge, and up the hill on the other side. Suzanne does not mind. Thérèse usually catches up to her before she crosses the bridge; and there are Brigette, Madeleine, Leonard, and Paul who go along as well.

Thérèse and Suzanne are good friends and sometimes visit each other. Thérèse's father keeps the store, a real country store with groceries, hardware, kerosene, dry goods, tobacco, and newspapers. Thérèse and Suzanne sit near each other in school, and both have been asked to see that the plants are watered and to keep small bouquets on the high shelf where the statue of the Blessed Virgin stands. In the winter, when the flowers are gone, they make paper flowers, or bouquets of bits of spruce or twigs with red berries.

Sister Marie teaches the girls of Suzanne's grade. The boys are in another room, and are taught by Sister Catherine.

Most of the girls wear either dark-blue or black dresses to school, with narrow turned-back cuffs and collars of fine white muslin or embroidery.

One of the first things Sister Marie teaches in history is the story of the French explorer who discovered Canada. His name was Jacques Cartier. The Gaspé Peninsula is that part of Canada that lies north of Maine and reaches out into the Gulf of St. Lawrence. It was on the Gaspé Coast that Jacques Cartier landed in 1534. Here he and his men erected a great cross with a shield on which were the lilies of France.

Suzanne likes to think about the time he sailed into the bay right near where she lives. It was a warm day in July, so warm that Cartier called it the Bay of Heat.

After that, for many years, fishermen from France and from the Isles of Jersey and Guernsey, just off the coast of France, came over for the great catches of cod and herring on the banks or fishing beds near the Gaspé

Coast, returning home when the season was over. Little by little, some of them stayed on the coast of the new land, and most of the people who live there now are their descendants.

That was more than four hundred years ago, but the people who live on the Gaspé Coast still speak the French language. Some of them learn to speak English, now, as Suzanne does, but the songs Suzanne sings are the same ones the sailors used to sing. Even the fiddler's tunes are the same ones that set people to jigging a hundred years ago.

When lessons were over for the day, Sister Marie snapped her *claquette*,—little wooden clapper,—and all the girls rose from their seats. She clicked it again, and they all knelt, with hands palm to palm, and said the closing prayer. The little claquette sounded again, and the girls rose from their knees, and Thérèse and Suzanne left quietly with the rest, two by two.

When they went outside the sky was black with clouds. But it is often cloudy on the coast, so the girls thought nothing of it and started on their way. Suddenly it began to rain in torrents. The girls ran on for a minute, then sought shelter. They ran up a lane to the nearest house, across the porch, and in the door. They were just about to cross the kitchen to the stove when they heard an angry voice from the other room. Thérèse's finger went to her lips, her eyes rolled as she looked at Suzanne whose shoulders were shaking with laughter.

They crept to the door as quietly as they could, opened it, and went out into the rain. They tiptoed across the porch and down the steps, then ran for all they were worth down the lane to the road. They didn't stop running till they were well out of sight of the house, then, all out of breath, they stood in the pouring rain and laughed until they ached. You see, the cottages along the road are much alike, and in their hurry to get out of the rain they had gone by mistake into the house of the Widow La Farge. No child *ever* goes into the widow's house! She is very odd and isn't fond of children, as are all the other women of the village. Why, there isn't a place in the village where the girls wouldn't feel welcome except the house of the Widow La Farge. If you stop in at Mama Pellettier's, she always has a piece of cake and a pleasant word for you; if you stop to see Madam Methot, perhaps she will just be taking the week's baking out of the brick oven under the little shed. She will ask you to come in and eat some fresh bread with wild strawberry jam. If you stop at the cabin of "Ol' Batees," he will not only give you a dish of raspberries with thick cream, but will get out his fiddle and play you a tune as well!

The rain stopped as suddenly as it had begun, but the sky was still overcast. The girls went bravely through the long dark bridge and up the road. Suzanne called "*Au r'voir*," good-by, as she turned in the lane, and Thérèse went on home.

Rogue, her dog, came bounding down the lane and, in his joy at seeing Suzanne, almost knocked her down, prancing along beside her, barking and wagging his tail. Aunt Eugénie was just coming in from feeding the chickens; she looked very funny in Uncle Jacques's old hat, with her apron full of vegetables she had gathered in the kitchen garden.

"You see," says Aunt Eugénie, "if we do not provide for the winter, then we have nothing to eat. The cold comes down and the snow. It fills all the roads; it covers all the fields. So we must save everything."

So she fills all the empty jars with vegetables, with fruits, and with *tête de fromage*, which is meat from the head of the pig. Sometimes when a hen is too old to lay, she cooks it, cuts it up, and puts that in jars too. There are always a few jars filled with delicious Gaspé salmon, as well. Then there is always something for a meal, even at the end of a long, cold winter; and how good it tastes!

Sometimes Aunt Eugénie puts currants with sugar and raisins in a great stone crock "from the old time" to make wine for the feast at Christmas. The feast is the supper after the Midnight Mass on Christmas Eve. And, oh, how Suzanne looked forward to it! Aunt Eugénie also stores away blocks of maple sugar to crumble for *crêpes suzette*, the thin egg pancakes which are so good for dessert.

"I will shell the peas as soon as I change my school dress," said Suzanne.

Uncle Jacques lighted his pipe and told Suzanne he would help her. André, Suzanne's brother, had the wood box filled, and they all settled themselves to shell peas, and to cut up carrots, beets, cabbages, and snap beans for soup stock. The clean glass jars stood in rows waiting to be filled, and Aunt Eugénie had found caps and rubbers to fit them. The packed jars would be put into the wash boiler and cooked a long time.

When Suzanne had begun her task, Ol' Batees came in bringing a basket of high-bush cranberries that he had gathered. Aunt Eugénie is always sending little things over to him—a cake, a kettle of soup, or some fresh bread—because he lives alone. So, when the little red berries are ripe in the wood, he always brings some for Aunt Eugénie to make jelly.

Everyone is always glad to see Ol' Batees; his big hearty laugh fills the house, and somehow he sets everyone else to laughing, too. He always has some news, or a story to tell. Sometimes it is just gossip.

Aunt Eugénie said, "Sit down, sit down!" She got up to make room for him. Uncle Jacques wanted him to take his place, but André and Suzanne begged him to sit between them on the bench.

"So," he chuckled, "it is not enough that I work all day for nothing; you must make me work all night too?" He sat down with André on one side and Suzanne on the other, and, heaped up before him, a great pile of peas to shell.

"Now," Ol' Batees began furiously to shell peas, "the last one to finish must tell a story, eh?"

"Oh, yes!" said Suzanne, as she slyly added another handful of peas to the pile in front of Ol' Batees. André saw her and, with a wink, added a few of his own. Ol' Batees pretended not to see and went on shelling the peas. The pods were so full that the peas popped all over the floor. There was a scramble to pick them up, and they almost upset the bench. What fun they had!

Ol' Batees started up a song in his rollicking voice, and in no time they were all singing and swaying their heads as they worked. They sang "Frères Jacques," that almost everyone knows, and "Au Clair de la Lune," which was one of Suzanne's favorite songs.

Then the children sang "On the Bridge at Avignon," and when they came to the "Rustique," Uncle Jacques joined in with the rest, his blue eyes twinkling with fun, and Ol' Batees not only roared out the melody, but must get up and do it with gestures. He danced, and bowed to the ladies, and "cut the pigeon wing." This is a fancy step that Ol' Batees knows well. Suzanne got up and danced with him, but laughed so hard she couldn't sing.

Ol' Batees finished up the song with "Suzanne, she shells the peas and cuts up all the vegetables!" and swung her around till her skirts stood out straight. Then, all out of breath, he sat down, mopping his head.

All the peas were shelled except a small pile in front of the place where Ol' Batees had been sitting! "*Eh-hein!* So, it is a trick you play on me, no?" How they all laughed!

Then, in the firelight, with Pouf the cat and Rogue the dog beside them, they all listened to Ol' Batees as he told a ghost story of the days long ago when the French first came to the Gaspé Peninsula.

Adapted

The Canadian Pioneers

REVEREND HUGH F. X. SHARKEY

This was, in days gone by, a wilderness,
   Dense-timbered hills and plains of rocky soil.
Behold, the far-flung dwellings of a nation
   Rise—monuments to human hand and toil.

Honor to them—the noble pioneers—
   Planting a country's flag on unknown sod,
Bearing aloft the crucifix of Christ
   To teach to savage men the love of God.

Day after day they toiled with ready zeal
   To fell the forest and to till the sod,
And set aside in simple faith a day
   When they would rest and give their thanks to God,

Who looked with pleasure on their frugal life,
   Blessed with His love their every, little way,
Ripened with sun and rain their growing fields,
   Smiled down upon the little ones at play.

No monument arises to their name,
   No testimony written by our hand;
Only, where once a wilderness had stood,
   Behold—the far-flung nations of the land.

Have you ever read the stories of Brer Fox and Brer Rabbit?
If you have,
you already know the humor and kindness of these stories
of the South that were told by beloved Uncle Remus.
If you do not know the famous folklore,
or if you do, laugh with

The Wonderful Tar Baby

JOEL CHANDLER HARRIS

For a long time Brer Fox had wanted to catch Brer Rabbit, but Brer Rabbit wouldn't be caught. At last, one fine day, Brer Fox had an idea. He got a chunk of tar and softened it with turpentine and made it into something that looked like a baby. Then he set this tar baby down by the side of the road and put a hat on its head and went away and hid in the bushes to see what would happen. He didn't have to wait long, for by and by Brer Rabbit came down the road—lippity-clippity, clippity-lippity, just as saucy as a jay-bird. Brer Fox lay low. Brer Rabbit came along until he saw the tar baby; then he suddenly stood up as if he was surprised. The tar baby just sat there and said nothing. Brer Fox lay low.

"Good morning," said Brer Rabbit to the tar baby. "Fine weather this morning."

The tar baby didn't say a word. Brer Fox lay low.

"How do you think you feel this morning?" said Brer Rabbit to the tar baby.

Brer Fox, in the bushes, just winked his eye slowly and lay low. The tar baby didn't say anything.

"What's the matter with you? Are you deaf?" said Brer Rabbit. "Because if you are, I can talk louder."

The tar baby kept still. Brer Fox lay low.

"You are stuck up. That's what you are!" said Brer Rabbit. "And I'm going to cure you of being stuck up. That's what I'm going to do."

Brer Fox chuckled softly, away down in his stomach. The tar baby said nothing.

"I'm going to teach you how to talk to respectable folks," said Brer Rabbit. "Take off that hat and say 'good morning.'"

The tar baby kept still. Brer Fox lay low.

Brer Rabbit kept on talking to the tar baby, and the tar baby kept on saying nothing, until, at last, Brer Rabbit drew back and—blip! he hit the tar baby on the side of the head. And that's where he made a mistake, because his fist stuck fast to the tar baby. He couldn't pull it away. The tar held him.

The tar baby kept still and Brer Fox lay low.

"If you don't let me go, I'll hit you again," said Brer Rabbit; and with that—biff! he hit him with the other hand. That stuck fast, too.

The tar baby said nothing. Brer Fox lay low.

"Let go, or I'll kick you!" said Brer Rabbit. The tar baby said nothing, but kept holding on tight. So Brer Rabbit kicked him with his right foot. That stuck fast, too.

"If I kick you with my other foot," shouted Brer Rabbit, "you'll think the lightning struck you."

The tar baby said nothing. Biff! he kicked the tar baby with his left foot; and his left foot stuck fast.

Then Brer Rabbit cried out that if the tar baby didn't let go, he would butt him in the stomach. So he butted him in the stomach; and his head stuck fast.

Just then Brer Fox sauntered out of the bushes, looking as innocent as you please.

"Good morning, Brer Rabbit," said he. "You look a little stuck up this morning." Then he lay down and rolled on the ground, and laughed and laughed until he couldn't laugh any more. By and by he said, "Well, I think I've got you this time, Brer Rabbit. Maybe not, but I think I have. You've been running around here and making fun of me for a long time, but I think you've got through now. You're always putting your nose into places where you have no business. Who asked you to come and get acquainted with that tar baby? And who got you so stuck up? You just jammed yourself up against that tar baby without waiting to be asked; and there you are, and there you'll stay until I gather up a brush pile and set fire to it; because I'm going to have you for dinner today."

Then Brer Rabbit was very humble. "I don't care what you do with me, Brer Fox," he said, "only don't throw me into that brier patch. Roast me, if you must, Brer Fox, but don't throw me into that brier patch."

"It's so much trouble to kindle a fire, that I expect I'll have to hang you," said Brer Fox.

"Hang me as high as you please, Brer Fox," said Brer Rabbit, "but don't throw me into that brier patch."

"I haven't any string," said Brer Fox, "so I expect I'll have to drown you."

"Drown me as deep as you please, Brer Fox," said Brer Rabbit, "but don't throw me into that brier patch."

Now Brer Fox thought if Brer Rabbit didn't want to be thrown into the brier patch, that was the very place where he should go. So he caught Brer Rabbit by the hind legs and threw him right into the middle of the brier patch. There was a great fluttering where Brer Rabbit struck the bushes, and Brer Fox waited to see what would happen.

By and by he heard somebody call, and away up the hill he saw Brer Rabbit, sitting cross-legged on a log, combing the tar out of his hair with a chip. Then Brer Fox knew he had been fooled.

Brer Rabbit shouted to him, "I was born and brought up in a brier patch, Brer Fox." And with that he skipped off, as lively as you please.

Many times you have held a sea shell to your ear
and have listened to its strange and mysterious sound.
Amy Lowell tells you in the poem that follows
what that roaring sound says to her.

Sea Shell

AMY LOWELL

Sea Shell, Sea Shell,
   Sing me a song, O please!
A song of ships, and sailor men,
   And parrots, and tropical trees,
Of islands lost in the Spanish Main
Which no man ever may find again,
Of fishes and corals under the waves,
And sea horses stabled in great green caves.
Sea Shell, Sea Shell,
Sing of the things you know so well.

If Once You Have Slept on an Island

RACHEL FIELD

If once you have slept on an island,
   You'll never be quite the same;
You may look as you looked the day before
   And go by the same old name.

You may bustle about in street and shop;
   You may sit at home and sew,
But you'll see blue water and wheeling gulls
   Wherever your feet may go.

You may chat with the neighbors of this and that
   And close to your own fire keep,
But you'll hear ship whistle and lighthouse bell
   And tides beat through your sleep.

Oh, you won't know why, and you can't say how
   Such change upon you came,
But—once you have slept on an island,
   You'll never be quite the same!

There have been many stories written about horses. None, though, ever stirred its readers so deeply as the tale told by the gentle dark horse of Birtwick, who was called

Black Beauty

ANNA SEWELL

The first place that I can well remember was a large pleasant meadow with a pond of clear water in it. Some shady trees leaned over it, and rushes and water-lilies grew at the deep end. Over the hedge on one side we looked into a plowed field, and on the other we looked over a gate at our master's house, which stood by the roadside; at the top of the meadow was a clump of fir trees, and at the bottom a running brook overhung by a steep bank.

While I was young I ran by my mother's side by day, and at night I lay down close by her. When it was hot we used to stand by the pond in the shade of the trees, and when it was cold, we had a nice warm shed.

As soon as I was old enough to eat grass, my mother used to go out to work in the daytime and came back in the evening.

There were six young colts in the meadow besides me; they were older than I was; some were nearly as large as grown-up horses. I used to run with them and had great fun; we used to gallop all together round and round the field, as hard as we could go. Sometimes we had rather rough play, for they would frequently bite and kick as well as gallop.

One day, when there was a good deal of kicking, my mother whinnied to me to come to her, and then she said, "I wish you to pay attention to what I am going to say to you. The colts who live here are very good colts, but they are cart-horse colts, and, of course, they have not learned manners. You have been well bred and well born; your father has a great name in these parts, and your grandfather won the cup two years at the Newmarket races; your grandmother had the sweetest temper of any horse I ever knew, and I think you have never seen me kick or bite. I hope you will grow up gentle and good, and never learn bad ways. Do your work with a good will, lift your feet up well when you trot, and never bite or kick even in play."

I have never forgotten my mother's advice. I knew she was a wise old horse, and our master thought a great deal of her. Her name was Duchess, but he often called her Pet.

Our master was a good, kind man. He gave us good food, good lodging, and kind words; he spoke as kindly to us as he did to his little children. We were all fond of him, and my mother loved him very much. When she saw him at the gate, she would neigh with joy and trot up to him. He would pat and stroke her and say, "Well, old Pet, and how is your little Darkie?" I was a dull black, so he called me Darkie; then he would give me a piece of bread, which was very good, and sometimes he brought a carrot for my mother. All the horses would come to him, but I think we were his favorites.

My mother always took him to the town on a market day in a light gig.

There was a plowboy, Dick, who sometimes came into our field to pick blackberries from the hedge. When he had eaten all he wanted, he would have, what he called, fun with the colts, throwing stones and sticks at them to make them gallop. We did not much mind him, for we could gallop off; but sometimes a stone would hit and hurt us.

One day he was at this game and did not know that the master was in the next field; but he was there, watching what was going on. Over the hedge he jumped in a snap, and catching Dick by the arm, he gave him such a box on the ear as made him roar with the pain and surprise. As soon as we saw the master, we trotted up nearer to see what went on.

"Bad boy!" he said, "bad boy! to chase the colts. This is not the first time, nor the second, but it shall be the last—there—take your money and go home, I shall not want you on my farm again." So we never saw Dick any more. Old Daniel, the man who looked after the horses, was just as gentle as our master, so we were well off.

When I was two years old I was beginning to grow handsome; my coat had grown fine and soft and was bright black. I had one white foot, and a pretty white star on my forehead. I was thought very handsome; my master would not sell me till I was four years old; he said lads ought not to work like men, and colts ought not to work like horses till they were quite grown up.

When I was four years old, Squire Gordon came to look at me. He examined my eyes, my mouth, and my legs; he felt them all down; and then I had to walk and trot and gallop before him; he seemed to like me, and said, "When he has been well broken in, he will do very well." My master said he would break me in himself, as he should not like me to be frightened or hurt, and he lost no time about it, for the next day he began.

Everyone may not know what breaking in is; therefore I will describe it. It means to teach a horse to wear a saddle and bridle and to carry on his back a man, woman, or child; to go just the way they wish, and to go quietly. Besides this, he has to learn to wear harness, and to stand still while it is put on; then to have a cart fixed behind him, so that he cannot walk or trot without dragging it after him; and he must go fast or slow, just as his driver wishes. He must never start at what he sees, nor speak to other horses, nor bite, nor kick, nor have any will of his own; but always do his master's will, even though he may be very tired or hungry. But the worst of all is, when his harness is once on, he may neither jump for joy nor lie down for weariness. So you see, this breaking in is a great thing.

I had of course long been used to a halter and a headstall, and had to be led about in the field and lanes quietly, but now I was to have a bit and a bridle. My master gave me some oats as usual, and after a good deal of coaxing he got the bit into my mouth and the bridle fixed, but it was a nasty thing! Those who have never had a bit in their mouths cannot think how bad it feels. A great piece of cold, hard steel, as thick as a man's finger, is pushed into one's mouth, between one's teeth and over one's tongue, with the ends coming out at the corner of your mouth, and held fast there by straps over your head, under your throat, round your nose, and under your chin; so that in no way in the world can you get rid of the nasty hard thing. It is very bad! yes, very bad! at least I thought so; but I knew my mother always wore one when she went out, and all horses did when they were grown up; and so, what with the nice oats, and what with my master's pats, kind words, and gentle ways, I soon learned to wear my bit and bridle willingly.

Next came the saddle, but that was not half so bad. My master put it on my back very gently, whilst old Daniel held my head. He then made the girths fast under my body, patting and talking to me all the time. Then I had a few oats, then a little leading about. This he did every day till I began to look for the oats and the saddle. At length, one morning my master got on my back and rode me round the meadow on the soft grass. It certainly did feel queer; but I must say I rather felt proud to carry my master, and as he continued to ride me a little every day, I soon became used to it.

The next unpleasant business was putting on the iron shoes. That, too, was very hard at first. My master went with me to the smith's forge, to see that I was not hurt or frightened. The blacksmith took my feet in his hand one after the other and cut away some of the hoof. It did not pain me, so I stood still on three legs till he had done them all. Then he took a piece of iron the shape of my foot, and clapped it on, and drove some nails through the shoe quite into my hoof, so that the shoe was firmly on. My feet felt very stiff and heavy, but in time I got used to it.

And now having got so far, my master went on to break me to harness. There were more new things to wear. First, a stiff, heavy collar just on my neck, and a bridle with great side-pieces against my eyes called blinkers, and blinkers indeed they were, for I could not see on either side, but only straight in front of me. Next there was a small saddle with a nasty stiff strap that went right under my tail; that was the crupper. I hated the crupper—to have my long tail doubled up and poked through a strap was almost as bad as the bit. I never felt more like kicking, but of course I could not kick such a good master, and so in time I got used to everything and could do my work as well as my mother.

I must not forget to mention one part of my training, which I have always considered a very great advantage. My master sent me for two weeks to a neighboring farmer's, who had a meadow which was skirted on one side by the railway. Here were some sheep and cows, and I was turned in among them.

I shall never forget the first train that went by. I was feeding quietly near the fence which separated the meadow from the railway, when I heard a strange sound at a distance. Before I knew whence it came—with a rush and a clatter, and a puffing out of smoke—a long black train of something flew by and was gone almost before I could draw my breath. I turned and galloped to the further side of the meadow as fast as I could go, and there I stood snorting with astonishment and fear. In the course of the day many other trains went by, some more slowly. These drew up at the station close by and sometimes made an awful shriek and groan before they stopped. I thought it very dreadful, but the cows went on eating very quietly and hardly raised their heads as the black frightful things came puffing and grinding past.

For the first few days I could not feed in peace, but as I found that this terrible creature never came into the field, or did me any harm, I paid no attention to it. Very soon I cared as little about the passing of a train as the cows and sheep did.

Since then I have seen many horses very much frightened at the sight or sound of a steam engine; but thanks to my good master's care, I am as fearless at railway stations as in my own stable.

Now if anyone wants to break in a young horse well, that is the way.

My master often drove me in double harness with my mother because she was steady and could teach me how to go better than a strange horse. She told me the better I behaved, the better I should be treated, and that it was wisest always to do my best to please my master; "but," said she, "there are a great many kinds of men; there are good, thoughtful men like our master, that any horse may be proud to serve; but there are bad, cruel men, who never ought to have a horse or dog to call their own. Besides, there are a great many foolish men, vain, ignorant, and careless, who never trouble themselves to think; these spoil more horses than all, just for want of sense. They don't mean it, but they do it for all that. I hope you will fall into good hands; but a horse never knows who may buy him, or who may drive him. It is all a chance for us, but still I say, do your best wherever it is and keep up your good name."

It was early in May when there came a man from Squire Gordon's, who took me away to the Hall at Birtwick. My master said, "Good-by, Darkie; be a good horse and always do your best." I could not say "good-by," so I put my nose into his hand. He patted me kindly, and I left my first home.

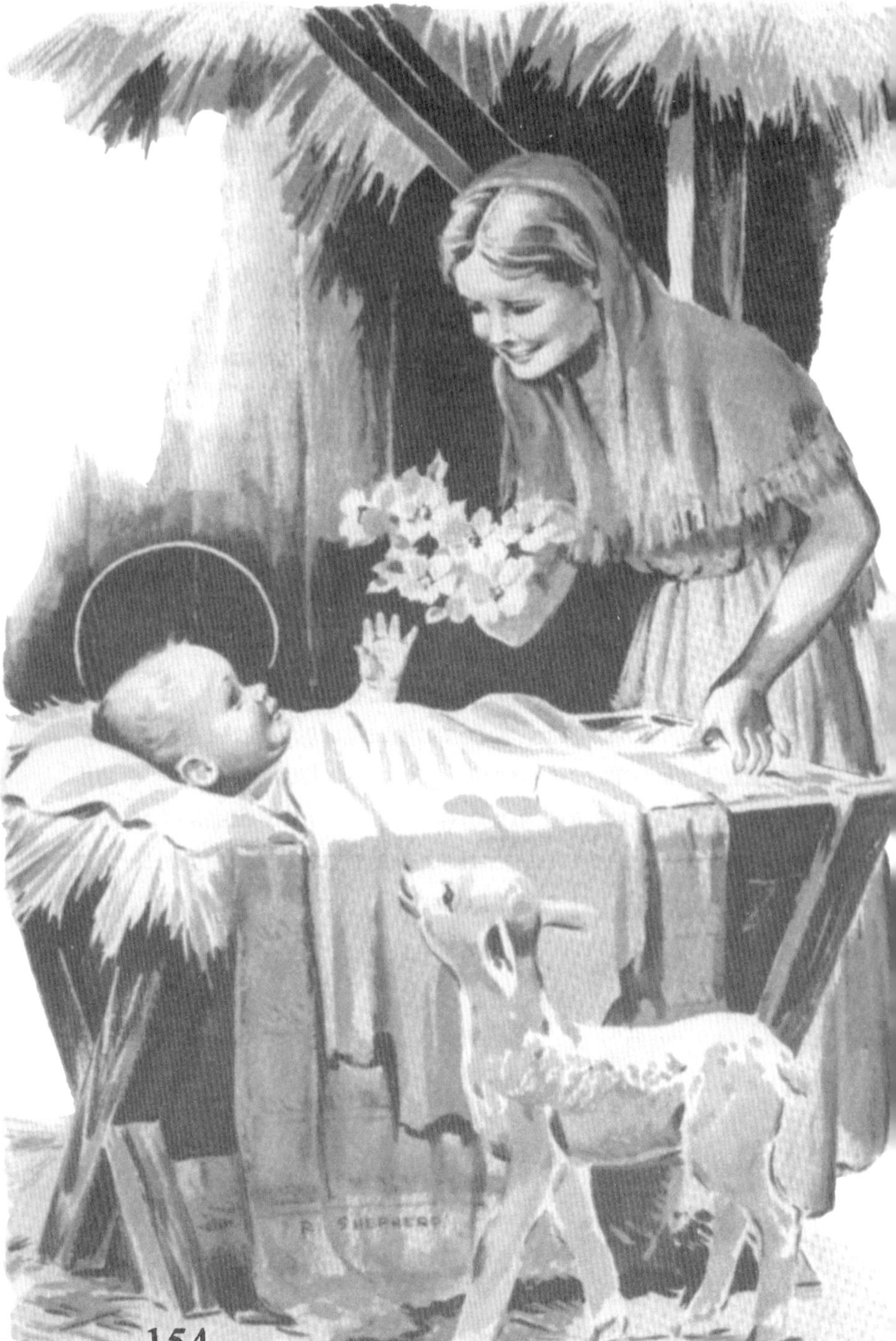

The Legend of the Christmas Rose

Though we may never see
the soft, rolling hills
of the Holy Land;
never see the green vineyards,
the blue thistles, the yellow mimosa
along the holy roads;
there is a legend of Bethlehem
that belongs to all time—
it is the story of the Christmas rose.

In the days of Herod,
when Jesus was born,
behold, out of the east
came the Wise Men,
for they had seen the Star;
and they came to worship Him.
They entered the manger
where the Child lay,
and fell down and adored Him,
offering royal gifts of gold
and frankincense
and myrrh.

At the door of the manger,
in the softness of the night,
in the clouds of royal incense,
stood a weeping child,
filled with wonder

at the birth of Jesus,
but sorrowful because she carried
no rare or beautiful gift
to offer to the Child of Mary.

She wept, and suddenly,
a light shone around her,
and an angel spoke,
"Weep not," the angel said,
"for thy gift shall be
the loveliest of all."

The angel smiled,
and then the ground
was white with roses,
and the child knelt
and gathered the blossoms
and ran with them into the manger.

He reached for the roses,
the Christmas roses,
and, for the child,
who had wept
because she had nothing to offer
as token of her love,
the Babe of Bethlehem smiled,
and His smile was brighter
than the Star
that had led all manner of men
to the poor, cold, humble place
of His holy birth.

Bells in the Country

ROBERT NATHAN

Bells in the country,
  They sing the heart to rest
When night is on the highroad
  And day is in the west.

And oh! they came to my house
  As soft as beggars shod,
And brought it nearer heaven,
  And maybe nearer God.

A Wish for Laughter

BRIAN O'HIGGINS

Wherever you may fare
On the highways of the world,
May no eye of anger look at you,
No shaft of hate be hurled,
May old sorrow flee before you,
Its gloomy banner furled;
In your footsteps
May sunshine follow after.

When you travel up the high hills
Or travel down again,
When you work or when you play
In crowded haunts of men,
When you rest in the quiet
Of some dreamy, silent glen,
In your heart
Be the merry lilt of laughter!